WORKING KNOWLEDGE

PETER KRÁL

WORKING KNOWLEDGE

Translated from the French
by Frank Wynne

PUSHKIN PRESS
LONDON

English translation © Frank Wynne 2008

First published in French as
Notions de base 2005
© Editions Flammarion 2005

This edition first published in 2008 by
Pushkin Press
12 Chester Terrace
London N1 4ND

British Library Cataloguing in Publication Data:
A catalogue record for this book is available
from the British Library

ISBN 978 1 901285 73 4

All rights reserved. No part of this publication may be
reproduced, stored in a retrieval system or transmitted in
any form or by any means, electronic, mechanical,
photocopying, recording or otherwise,
without prior permission in writing from
Pushkin Press

Cover: From the film *Coffee & Cigarettes*
© 2003 Smokescreen Inc.
Courtesy of Jim Jarmusch

Frontispiece: Petr Král
© Didier Pruvot Editions Flammarion

Set in 10.5 on 15 Monotype Baskerville
by Alma Books Ltd
and printed in Great Britain
by TJ International

For Danka

It is our blindness, existential blindness, which makes the world around us so mysterious. In his discreet way, Petr Král lifts the veil. We know what the word 'smoking' means, but we were incapable of seeing what 'smoking' means in concreto, *how these insignificant, automatic gestures bind us to the world or how they make it possible for us to stray from it as evinced by the story of Lenin, a non-smoker, asking Trotsky for a cigarette so that, for a moment, he might forget the revolution. We know what 'solitude' means, but our existential blindness made it impossible for us to realise that the 'chamber of solitude' is separated by a flimsy, resonant door from the room where the party raucously rages on. How many times, late at night, have we glanced towards a woman as she leaves a party alone, only to forget everything that glance contained an instant later. It is surprising that these everyday situations, as infinitesimal as they are elemental are so little influenced by the singularity of individual psychology. They wait for us, they subdue us. This strange and beautiful existential encyclopaedia of the everyday is a lesson in modesty inflicted upon our sense of self.*

MILAN KUNDERA

Coffee

YOU STEP OUT into a Saturday morning, rising late you slip between slivers of time with the gentle imprecision that only the most genial of mornings affords; only rejoining the living—as if obliquely—when you plant your elbows on the bar of a café to order a coffee which you will drink as, with half-an-eye, you watch the hazy backwash of the street outside. To then let yourself venture out to meet yourself, propelled by the scalding liquid, unexpectedly real, which moves over your tongue and slips down your throat with a residue of night, is, despite your offhand manner, to put in an honourable appearance at the very heart of the vague.

The Shirt

For Milan Sohulz

A CLEAN SHIRT is a second—a better—skin, its rustlings and flutterings swell the breathing of the epidermis with which we are gifted once and for all and which the shirt celebrates and flatters almost lovingly. The all-encompassing day itself seems to caress us as it slips beneath the fabric with the breeze; to say goodbye to a shirt that has served its time will stir in us almost the same heartbreak as a mistress. The shirt, in other words, is much closer to us than the coat in whose pockets, as in the vast world, we are all too often already lost. Hardly more auspicious are the trousers to which, each morning, we plough our weary way as to a railway station.

Dawn

For Christian Hubin

THOSE WHO SAY they love mornings usually bestow their affection on an already advanced hour, one sunny and confident enough to serve merely as a pristine backdrop for the sundry activities of the day. By contrast, rare indeed are those who love the dawn, a washed-out, ashen period in which all things are reborn into doubt, shrink back from the threshold of non-being to start again from square one; a period in which all things absorbed by a common nothingness, become eloquent—become heralds—in their mute trembling. The bone stripped to the bone, suddenly revealed in all its lividity.

The journalists who came to Mexico to interview Luis Buñuel on the eve of his death say that the deaf old fox would sit on his terrace at dawn, gazing at a tree swaying in the breeze, tilting his head to listen to the rustling of leaves as to a wellspring; and to judge by the elated expression on his face—both satisfied and perfectly amazed—this slight rustling was sufficient to relieve him of all unnecessary burdens. Was he thinking at that moment of his great friend Lorca who, years before, had suddenly seen his limitations give ground before him as his last sigh melted into the murmurs and the brightening half-light of some olive grove?

Spectacle

A NEW, EACH MORNING, astonished witness to the spectacle of the ashtray, the glasses and the decanter, unmoving, marking out the flatlands of the table.

Le Petit Déjeuner, Breakfast

DESPITE THE KINSHIP between their names which, in French, associates the morning with the midday meal, *le petit déjeuner*—the continental breakfast—is distinct from the *le déjeuner*: the sweetness of jams and of honey added to the crustiness of bread, the roundness of the bowl of coffee and the reassuring depth of its crater into which, as we drink, we plunge our faces as if for a moment we might return to the nocturnal bed, perpetuating each morning a memory of childhood and of the maternal protection we knew there. More akin to a 'real' meal, the English breakfast, in which bacon and eggs form a virile complement to the innocence of cornflakes or porridge, is also more adult; whereas *le petit déjeuner* breakfast, on the threshold of the day, creates a haven of intimacy to cling to before braving the morning—whose memory, in fact, will protect us in the thick of it—*breakfast* compels us to reclaim the bearing of a conqueror, pushes us to brave the mass, the fabric of the real through the steadfastness of smoked bacon and the warm flow of an egg yolk. If what sustains us in the first is the memory of a nanny singing, recording our lives in the register of a noble lineage, the second makes it possible for us to defend ourselves against the status of orphan to which, each day, we return on waking.

Shaving

IN SHAVING OURSELVES, we put on a soapy white face as though to play the clown, the better to find beneath the foam his bare skin; in a brief, eternal parenthesis we stand on the edge of time itself, preparing to plunge back in. Just as at the moment of waking we have the freshest and most incisive ideas of the day, better yet: as we shave we know *everything*. While the body is preoccupied with its own care, turning its attention to its slightest tale, the mind takes to the wing like a peripatetic bee, flies round the world seeking out its hidden reserves. An imperceptible quiver in the air or in ourselves, something and nothing, will determine whether the shave is a success or a failure—just as it determines the act of love which at this instant, with the aid of a razor, we try to practise with ourselves. Something and nothing, this breeze that lightly brushes the cheek, to finish, with a drop of cologne, like a last shudder of the chasm which, by shaving, we have once more managed to cross.

Morning

For Jan Šulc

SITTING AT A SCHOOL DESK, WE TRIED hard to concentrate, sometimes actually listening to what was being said. But little by little, our thoughts, just as surely as with our eyes, slipped towards the still-open window convinced that out there, somewhere, we were missing something; thinking about everything, about nothing. We were not, but rather attentive to the vastness of thought itself which encompassed even our floating selves; even the teacher's words made sense only against the backdrop of the distant murmur of the day.

This is why we are never closer to a state of grace than on those mornings when we lie in bed, half-awake, allowing ribbons of thought and itinerant dreams to drift idly through our minds. We are as yet no more than pure potential, like the day itself as it begins, we come and go within ourselves, sending out feelers and drawing them back again, between the shadows and the flares of light which occasionally reach us from between the closed curtains; we stir up memories drawn from wisps of female flesh, faces and fond words only to allow them to sink back and drown. Barely conscious of our own existence, we savour it all the more completely, as we do the world around us. We defer the moment when we will begin reading; luxuriating in our longing for the book which waits for us and this matutinal frustration which will heighten our acuity allowing us to recognise each moderately well-turned phrase. We need only focus our attention a little and suddenly ideas, phrases, incisive remarks appear from the haze which hangs still in our minds, and it is from here, from the first, we feel our keenest lucidity.

Even when we finally pick up the book, we do not quite lose sight of the great trembling mass in which, just a moment before, we saw, amid the flickering light and shade, our library transformed, as if plunging endlessly into the teeming, dusty depths of the books, the manuscripts and the messages never written and those that are yet to come. We constantly put down one book only to get up and take down others, comparing them with the first, seeking in their pages some addendum, some new detail about what we have read. Sometimes, we spend the whole morning in the library, pacing the aisles of books, taking down first one book then another only to replace them having skimmed only a few short words. Far from wasting time, each attempt is like beginning a new life, boundless and immemorial. As we linger, leafing simultaneously through all the riches of the world, we too are eternal, unbounded; and here we would remain, though we were struck down by a thunderbolt, a book still open in our hands.

The Clock

CITIES WOULD BE INCOMPLETE without the clocks which appear suddenly, at a crossroads, towering above the unfurling wave of passers-by; but the reassurance the eye seeks in the clock face is something much greater than the right time. The gaze the clock face returns, open and serene from beyond the hands whose position, rather than indicating a specific time simply evokes a secret yawn in time—this clock face sustains us only by what is flat and neutral in its gaze; the time it indicates is merely that against which, limitless and slow, all existence is played out; the tranquil roundedness of the clock face, the position of the hands, remind us that we are in the world.

The space defined by many cities is revealed all the more clearly by being demarcated by clocks which, from one street corner to another, denote a different time (almost a different season)—without ever seeming wrong for each of the places over which they tower, each with its own bustle, its own pace. Indeed in exemplary fashion the clock atop a neighbourhood town hall in Bruxelles stubbornly persisted for many years in marking each moment with the same gesture, the hands coming together at the twelve; a symbol of the zero hour which, from the first, contains all others.

The Market

It would be rash to see the richness of a market in its merchandise. Though every morning a throng of stallholders set up in some small town and there spill forth a torrent of fabrics, cries, hurried footsteps among the fruits and the glassware on display, the colourful stalls bring to the scene only the fleeting richness of a mirage whose true goal is to vanish at the appointed hour. Only when as the awnings above the stalls have wilted, the flags flutter at half-mast as for some unexpected death, when the stallholders bend over identical piles of cardboard boxes into which the miscellany of objects has been reabsorbed do we realise that a market is to the small town what a dress is to a woman: a temporary veil which, when stripped away, reveals more clearly her radiant nakedness.

Above the drooping stalls, we begin to rediscover the stillness of the buildings, shutters half-closed on a fault-line of shadow, the emptiness of the town square begins to reappear beneath the debris, unfurling again its relaxed breathing only briefly belied by a scrap of newspaper wildly dancing. While the silhouette of a man in the middle of the square bending to tie his shoelaces calmly signals the start of a simultaneous race to the four corners of the afternoon—around the perimeter, through the mouths of doors once more unhindered in the heart of the town, the expanse begins once more to silently drink us in.

The Flight of Steps

IT TAKES ONLY AN INCLINE of a few degrees for the act of walking to take on a greater significance; every flight of stairs immediately heightens our action, reminding us that beyond the simple moving through space, walking is also a form of progress, a test to be accomplished by overcoming obstacles. Through the additional effort they require of us, steps also offer us the opportunity to experience the act of walking as an adventure and acquit ourselves heroically in our task as passers-by. Interrupting the orderly progress of the day to climb a flight of stairs immediately gives our walking purpose. The slow climb in the half-light of a house (even if it is our own house) becomes an adventure, a painstaking expedition where we can never know what lies in wait, can never truly anticipate our route: the surprises and the traps that wait for us—the stranger we meet on the way, the curved banister that slips beneath our fingers, the pitch or the width of the steps we struggle to climb. Instead of a last stair, we know that we shall be met at journey's end by pure illusion: a floating, formless step which may disappear beneath our feet or trip us like a piece of shadow suddenly made solid just as the time switch on the light clicks off and everything is plunged into darkness.

The people we encounter, inside a house or outside, as we climb a flight of steps, offer clues which we must carefully decipher the better to anticipate the remainder of our own journey. From their happy or anxious expressions we try to gauge what lies in wait, weighing each subtle nuance of gesture and expression—just as they weigh ours—reading in their faces our chances of attaining our goal. The heavy tread of a man squeezed into his raincoat inspires us to be more cautious—though not without relieving us of some part of our burden—in the quivering skirt of a young woman framed against the light walking briskly down towards us, we hear the murmur of an undiscovered kingdom of which she is the herald unless she is it's queen.

But now, having succeeded in climbing to the summit, we in turn are heading back downstairs where we will become pedestrians once more among the crowd. The descent lends all its weight to our success or our failure, adding a fateful drum roll to the latter just as it transforms the former into dazzling triumph, applauded by the clapping of the wind which whips round the stairwell. No sooner do we leave even a mundane office where we have dispatched some inconsequential task than the very act of stepping out into the street, having negotiated the stairs, is a glorious relief, a hard-won freedom—all the more so if, by chance, we should emerge into the clamour and bustle of a market.

As we climb a flight of steps, the most noble way to complete our task—and to pay tribute to the obstacle which the stairway represents—is to go back a step of two and glance down towards the bottom before taking the final step. To fully savour our success, we cannot separate it from the last step and the sigh which, at the top of the stairs, we heave, faced with our final task: going down again.

The Walking Stick

1

THE WALKING STICK IS SOMETHING MORE than a mere useful object; it is both a tool and a luxury that lends an elegance to the act of walking—even for the infirm and the elderly who appear to use it out of sheer necessity. In the way it makes his gait more sweeping, more dramatic, more expansive, the walking stick is to a man what the skirt is to a woman: a mitigation of, and a metaphysical extension to the body. This is why even a blind man, when he knows he is unobserved, will contentedly twirl his cane; the dandy's walking stick is both an accessory and a stick which spurs him on to walk with an exuberance in keeping with his appearance, to hone his nonchalance into a moral stance. A supplementary offering the walker support, a walking stick always traces a path beyond the ambit traced by the walker's feet; lifted by a hand, it points towards other possible goals, dropped back onto the pavement, it dispatches a cigarette butt with the assurance of a raptor. By turns, it presents two distinct but complementary facets, now the remoteness of a blind, unyielding substance, now the precision of a shaft of solid light which navigates unaided by the man who wields it. Ideally, it is both at once, a substance which is as lucent as it is solid capable of discerning one's *true destination* as one walks. Beneath the trees of an elegant avenue in a city centre, a place of habitation suddenly appear here, in the warmth of the afternoon, as the walking stick presses a layer of yellowing leaves against the pavement and casts a brilliant glimmer on the ground. Sometimes, in the early hours, what is walking stick and support is but the gleaming hiccup of a trumpeter soaring from the grooves of an old black LP record, to fleetingly score a defiant line through the night.

2

Set down in a corner, the walking stick continues its monologue in its owner's stead.

The Coat Rack

We feel a certain solidarity with its perfect nakedness under the temporary burden of our clownish finery.

The Hat

Lounging together in a shop window—a straw hat, frolicsome and summery, another, sceptical, in waterproof oilskin; a provincial Tyrolean hat and, next to it, a globe-trotting fedora—they comprise a whole world and an embryonic history in which, for as far as the eye can see, they mete out roles like cards. On the silver screen, the mysterious killer beneath one of the wave of hats unfurled along a rainy street, but which?

Each of those we have worn is a true love, a stranger and a lover. When we doff it on a street corner, in greeting or in simple deference to the afternoon, a wild infinity smiles fleetingly between head and hat.

The Train

No mode of transport has changed our knowledge of the world as much as the train. Before our train departs, we have already set off as the train on the adjoining track pulls out and, for a fleeting instant, makes us think that it is we who are moving—making us catch our breath, only to slump back into our ungainly body, motionless and subdued, as though we have come back before we left. Later, now on our way, the sky hurtles towards us, closer and more vivid than at any other time, from between the carriages of a passing train, where it clatters and quivers, a ribbon of shining metal. For as long as trains have existed, we know that we are always travelling in trains other than those in which we sit.

Level Crossings

All of us, surely, have gone to stare at level crossings and the trains as they flash past, envying the flagman who can spend his days in his signal box doing precisely that. This passing judgement is, of course, an illusion: the signalman does not see the trains as we see them precisely because, since he is always there, he does not have to come from elsewhere to watch the trains. Consequently he was oblivious even to the chaotic charm of the scene created by the signal box, the panoply of signals, the train tracks and the small garden in which points-levers blossom between the sunflowers.

For his part, he cannot begin to know how we feel, trapped in our cars behind the crossing gate, our journey suddenly interrupted by a train shunting us clear of its oblique path. As we wait for the train to pass, the world we have set out to discover flashes before our eyes in the carriage windows, individual tableaux of dispassionate dandies, *grandes dames* with their furrowed brows, an impassive ticket inspector; only much later in the kitchen of some remote hotel do we rejoin the world in the murmurs of the widowed hotelier who confides the recipe for his famous *ragoût* to us. Sometimes, a passing train is so memorable that it seems to suggest a world behind the world—as when a train briefly stops beside a level crossing and the factory chimney in the distance rises abruptly above the engine as though a part of it. Before we come to our senses, it almost seems as if the train is sweeping the chimney away with it to set it down in some distant valley, creating an utterly new landscape.

Trains

O UR TRAINS NO LONGER RUN ON STEAM, but their smoky breath still billows wider than the tracks they run on, beyond the route they follow.

The Toast

To my sister (and to Honza)

IN THE PRIME OF LIFE, a much admired Senior Registrar summons his disciples and his colleagues and informs them that he has been diagnosed with a serious illness which means that he is no longer allowed to smoke or drink alcohol. Then he lights a cigar, pops the champagne cork and proudly announces: "What is an eagle without his wings?", drains his glass in a single draught; he dies shortly afterwards. We have witnessed this same ritual many times, a man brandishing a bottle and a glass to underscore his message: the pilot safely returned to base pouring vodka shots and declaring that death can go to hell; the burnt-out trumpeter rising to his feet to a torrent of applause and, with a heavenly smile on his lips, assuring us we would live forever—even as he gazes towards the grave that already waits for him. These people showed us the way, showed us the end that waits for us all; their fall was the starting signal for our own journey, the band-leader's fatal plane crash lifted our glider into the wind.

Even today, when we raise our glasses in a toast, we are passing the baton, it is a gesture of compassion, of complicity between mortal men and it is a poisoned chalice. Inevitably one man clinks another's glass too hard, his drink spilling droplets on the other's shoulder—it's time for you to take your solo, to show how gracefully you can fall. Only then does he slide his glass against ours, raises it in salute, thus imparting as he does so a minimum of grace for our flight over the abyss.

The Barman

To Georges

"THE BARMAN," old P used to say from behind his bar, "the barman is there so that you have someone facing you." Neither confidant nor mere buffoon, the barman intercepts our gaze and politely returns it, preventing it from becoming lost in contemplation of the battery of bottles ranged behind the bar. But neither is he a simple stooge or a mirror of ourselves; a young Vietnamese man fills our glasses while we mock him gently in our language, he smiles and leaves us to our banter before turning to say, in perfect Czech, "My name is Táborsky". Only the fact that he is *other*, that he is different from us and from the idea we have of him, makes it possible for the barman to truly fulfil his role and offer us the necessary means to accept ourselves for what we are. It is for this reason—rather than from mere vanity or a need for entertainment—that a famous actor had his chauffeur serve his drinks every night; and it is this which explains why we spend an evening in New York out drinking with the tipsy barmaid behind the bar rather than with the friend who is sitting next to us. As we fill a page with our meaningless scribbles, we allow ourselves to appear out of its emptiness—out of our nothingness—to become our own barman.

The Journey

To Standa

When, having reached the brow of a hill and tired of pedalling, we let the bicycle freewheel downhill with a soothing rattle, we glimpsed the hidden face of the journey: not a mere duty but a feverish exaltation; beyond the drudgery of pedalling, it gifted us with a state of grace, the profound truth, the true goal which alone gave the journey meaning.

When Hodges[1] brings the alto sax to his lips and begins a solo, he is in no hurry to get somewhere, he allows himself to slide along, the exaltation of the journey sounding and resounding the rolling waves. Mozart, for his part, is pure release, a graceful gliding down the stairs which alone is sufficient to cause the rustling murmur, the whispers of chiffon and champagne in the room below to rise towards the ceiling. The exaltation is all the greater given that, like we as we cycle, both musicians are already swooping downhill; rather than stepping triumphantly into the arena, they have us sink, nobly but inexorably into them.

From the Train

To see the world from a train is not merely to see it from afar, but to see it differently. Beneath the surface details of a tree, a bend in the track, a bell tower we take in the passing landscape in its entirety just as we see the fugitive nature of its horizons; from a house beside the tracks another life leaps out at us, like a possibility we have spurned. A gardener stands with one hand on a fence, a naked man sharpens his knife by a side of beef hanging from a tree, we see their actions like so many invitations and reproaches which quickly freeze into omens engraved forever on our memories. Here and there, near a wayside cross or on a narrow bridge, we see ourselves from outside, finished figures set in a landscape.

The Door

THE DOOR IS THE BARRIER we set against intruders, against the outside world, but we constantly glance towards it, hoping for someone to get through: for the concierge to slide a letter underneath, for someone to knock, late at night. The confidence or apprehension with which we open the door will determine the nature of the message the caller brings, just as it will dictate the graveness or the gaiety of the time we will spend in his company. Still more important is the manner in which we open the door to leave, to step out into the world; the confidence with which we grasp the doorknob and cross the threshold determines in advance the outcome and the import of what awaits us outside, helps or hinders our arriving at a critical meeting, settling some trivial business matter, finding a good bistro. We hold the key to the door, but not to the day that lies beyond—which key remains constantly to be found, and we do so in the manner in which we cross the threshold.

Sometimes, we linger for a moment outside a shop or a studio, wondering whether or not to push the door and step inside; the secret hidden behind the door arouses both longing and misgiving, we worry that we will be caught up in some dark scheme or on the contrary be disappointed, we convince ourselves that, try as we might, the secret will elude us. We have good reason to think so, this would not be the first time we knew disappointment: we remember the time when the old grocer sold us pretzels riddled with worms, when no flash disturbed the half-light of the photographer's studio pervaded with a strong smell of urine; when shopkeepers blocked our view, bodily shielding the depths of their shop, innocently pretending there was no secret to be found. Yet even so, forging ahead, we push the door and step across the threshold—if only for a moment; if it feels as though we are stepping into nowhere, this could well be what it means to live, simply pushing open a door and stepping inside—into someone else's house, or merely into the next room. Even at home, we can sometimes speed the day along simply by stepping into the kitchen, into an empty room; perhaps the hoary joke about the Russian forerunner of television which consisted of moving a painting from one room to another, has some deeper meaning and harbours some essential lesson in the art of living. Visiting friends in summer, we push open the door to the guest room—furnished but unoccupied—and in its silence, an unfamiliar memory of our hosts as of ourselves rises to meet us, a memory which extends our stay here into some new space.

As we push to open their doors, rooms offer a certain resistance, emphasise their difference, defend it so fiercely sometimes that they prove to be more other than expected; the looming body in the next room sits up in bed like a corpse; in the darkness, even a woman we know intimately may push us away suddenly like a stranger, murmuring that she is not alone. Sometimes we knock on someone's door and get no reply, though we are sure they are expecting us; they have betrayed us, their door stands closed and inside they are partying without us, all our friends gathered together to betray us. Even when we stand before our own door, we do not always know what waits inside; sometimes, we find ourselves on the doorstep with no key, our humiliation all the greater because we have brought it on ourselves. As we shamefacedly wonder what we have done to deserve this, wonder with whom we are betraying ourselves inside, the familiar yet inaccessible apartment we nostalgically wander through in our minds already seems remote and strange, like a room set aside for guests.

The Wastepaper Basket

To Jan Vladislav

A NOBLER VARIANT ON THE DUSTBIN into which we drop the base, the stinking, the baser parts of our luxuries, the wastepaper basket is almost a friend; closer to us even than the small bathroom rubbish bin which allows us to check our availability for the coming day when, from a distance, we try to pitch some small object into it. The wastebasket stands by us through the day, prosaically yet patiently, ever ready to gulp down some scrap, some document that has ceased to interest us: torn envelopes, useless printouts, out-of-date messages and memos, drafts of letters and empty cigar boxes. Objects we have disowned even before we have thrown them away; we sometimes catch a glimpse of them in the wastebasket as we nod off, an aerial view, as if from a distant plane. (But what is it that suddenly, in mid-afternoon, impels the lead pencil stub to dive so deliberately into the wastebasket?)

If we are later forced, reluctantly, to rush back to the wastebasket to humbly search for some scrap of paper which has inadvertently found its way there, we feel it as a profound humiliation—all the more so since the wastebasket now offers us a single message like an unspoken truth: is the reality of our existence not mirrored in these things we have so confidently discarded, the naked, faded stuff of empty boxes, torn envelopes, pencil stubs and pages of scribbled corrections? And to cap it all, just as we angrily attempt to stuff everything back into the wastebasket, we discover that so perfect, so precise was the edifice previously formed little by little, patiently and humbly, by simple accretion over the course of days that it no longer fits. It is as if this sculpture of rubbish which, now rebuilt, stands frozen and precise—is our one true monument. At night, against the darkened window, it looks almost beautiful …

The Sneeze

OUR EVERY SNEEZE surprises us, like an unexpected invitation and an encouragement, but to what? Perhaps we should acknowledge, in broad daylight, our constant dissatisfaction and immediately transcend our limitations—all the more easily since we have been caught unawares—the limitations of bodies and those of the space bestowed upon us. And instantly we cleave the air and the sneeze propels us forward, with a firmness equivalent to its force; true, we slump back into ourselves, though less dissatisfied now. When racked by a bout of sneezing in the middle of the night, as we drain a last glass, are we in fact regretting the fact that our daytime sneeze did not propel us further still?

Laughter

WHEN WAS THE FIRST TIME we *genuinely* laughed? From the cradle, we knew how to cry and from the first could do so bitterly, with heartfelt desolation. To learn to laugh, however, we first had to make our way in the world, our childhood giggles were merely a sign, like a vague promise of things to come. Perhaps because laughter is born of our contact with a wider world, of our first conflicts with others, our first firm friends, our first social blunders—as though laughter can flourish only in the space carved out by our entry into society, in which laughter carves for itself a further space.

Only laughter has us in its grip so that it can make us truly inhabit the whole world. The peal of laughter that reaches us from the street or from the back of a bar is simply a siren song; the life, the world, it incites us to explore, shimmer above it like a passage we must navigate, in whose melody we seek only the key. By contrast, the laughter which shakes us when we are alone or in the company of others is nothing more than a grand *rejection of keys*, opening us indefinitely in every sense, its power all the greater since what it suddenly reveals is simply the impossibility of existence: we are not laughing at a joke but at reality itself, caught *in flagrante delicto*, its secret farce, the clumsy traps it sets each day to ensnare itself.

We, too, struggle with such traps, we long to declare our love, but hold our tongues; yet it is precisely through laughter that we are able to see the world more clearly, from both near and far as though, from some distant shore, we were relishing the sight of our own shipwreck. Laughter, which is both knowledge and release, reconciles us with our finitude and erases its limits; though it never ceases to shake us, we become almost immortal, the anxiety which brought it on dissipates into a boundless wonder which feeds upon itself, bringing fresh bursts of hilarity until we all but die laughing.

Relief

T̲ʜᴇ ᴜʀɢᴇɴᴛ ɴᴇᴇᴅ ᴛᴏ ʀᴇʟɪᴇᴠᴇ ᴏᴜʀꜱᴇʟᴠᴇꜱ spurs us to a greater confrontation. Stepping from a car beside a buzzing meadow or interrupting our descent, stop-swinging our skis on a bend, we momentarily step outside the flow of time, of events; in our tête-à-tête with nature we are also gauging our chances of conquering it. We pierce it with a liquid line, but the landscape rears up suddenly more solid, hemming us in like a block of silence, curious and cunning—the blades of grass, the crystals of snow glittering at our feet stretch out to the horizon towards which we now lift our gaze.

When, in summer, we step out into a restaurant courtyard to go and relieve ourselves in the toilet at the far end, the wine which burbles and gurgles inside us rushes forward to greet the world and attunes us to the muffled roar of the city, as we stand here waiting in the wings, with the evening stretched out before us and our partners-in-crime waiting back in the restaurant, a city which invites us to join some greater party, the one true party. When we return, our windswept expression is enough to alert our friends; there is no need—like the barroom philosopher at Hasek's—to lecture them about the night sky which hangs, unbeknownst to them, above their heads.

When, staying with friends, we step outside on a warm night to urinate in front of their house, the whole landscape, filled with scents, tremors, murmurs, creates a shifting bed for our thin stream; it surges towards us as though to embrace us, swelling around us to the starry vault, buoyed by the calm breath of the departed who are sleeping behind the yawning windows of the house and those long since departed whose bass drone, in turn, buoys them up. As it flows out of us, we gloriously recall an entire, singular, life; but if someone at that moment should ask our name, we would be utterly unable to answer.

The Dot and the Trail

To Ivan Wernisch

AS WE PUFF ON A CIGARETTE, standing in the night on the verge of a road, we are no more than an incandescent dot in the landscape; that which kept us company a moment before, suddenly flickers away, leaving nothing but a glowing trail. This smouldering point is also a target; he who lingers too long here awaits his fate like an unstoppable bullet—though perhaps it will be pure accident: he will be struck down by a meteor or a passing firefly and die foolishly like a bystander gunned down on the last day of the war by a mistrustful soldier. The glowing trail that follows is not simply a prolongation of the dot but erases the dot, drawing it across the landscape, tracing an empty wake upon the darkness. In doing so, not only does it dodge the sniper's bullet; but unlike the bullet, the trail has no target, its only goal the arc it traces across some glade—the very antithesis of the dot—making it something between a firefly in the grass and a distant star. It is an aspiration rather than a target, the muted quiver of an angel's wing; he who would seek it out disappears, little by little, into himself, like a jazzman suddenly tossing his cigarette into the darkness to launch into a solo. When, on the edge of the forest, a poet friend runs from the taxi driver he has no intention of paying he is transformed into a glowing trail of no fixed abode; the furious taxi driver immediately freezes as though he were already home.

Voices

IN THE HEART OF SUMMER in the heart of the city, the voices of diners, the tinkling of wine glasses and plates, of cutlery, reaches us through the trees, reverberating through the night, the bustle of the dining room behind the window spreading through space. These voices mingle with the rustle of the leaves, flickering like human stars between the branches and in the urban night evoking the memory of an old-fashioned rustic hospitality, some sunlit bucolic idyll to which we might return, towards which, like fascinating fireflies, the voices point the way. So bewitched are we by these sounds, these voices, that we are tempted to follow them, but we cannot, since they do not belong to a particular place, not even to the room whence they came, they belong only to the cloud they create, the ethereal floating island which carries them deep into the night, and with them the glow of the dining room. A simple insubstantial breath, no heavier than the fleeting flare of light which reflected into our house from the window opposite, like a flimsy rustle of summer dresses.

The best way to join the voices would be to invite the diners to come outside and stand where we stand, listening to themselves: but that, sadly, is impossible. At best, we might fashion a paper plane from a fine piece of Bristol card and launch it towards the dining room in the hope that, having circled the table, gleaming in the light of the chandeliers and eliciting appreciative sighs from all present, it might come back to the street and land at our feet like some message from those inside; but we would not dare to go so far. Perhaps at least, we think, our rapt fascination with this window might coax the dinner guests out onto the balcony during a storm where they might have the unexpected good fortune to witness a fireball as it passes. Something for which they might thank us by sending out onto the balcony the most beautiful woman in the party—if only to demonstrate how to use a lifejacket.

The Balcony

The room at our backs is hectic with clamour and light—the party is a roaring success—yet the balcony to which we have retreated is deep in shadow, even the shouts and catcalls from within echo only weakly. Nor are we necessarily alone: nearby, two unknown bodies rub against one another mewing plaintively. Whereas inside, we simply threaded our way through the partygoers as through a crowded waiting room, out here on the balcony, we feel, as never before, the romance of the world in which we play our part—be it only the role of a mute witness. Every whispered confidence out on the balcony is of paramount importance, though we will not remember them, they will remain forever lost in the darkness which encroaches on the balcony and in the night beyond over which we tower—perhaps *because* they are important.

The night-time conversation we overhear between two men on the balcony of the Central Committee, resonates as confused echoes around the quiet of some public square of a town we are merely passing through. The whispered confidences broadcast from this grandstand are perhaps no more than the trivial gossip of two night-watchmen; yet the moment they are uttered, they are irrevocable and fraught with consequences merely because these men went out onto the balcony to say it.

Light

I*n the room bathed* in the glare of a ceiling light, everything is frozen by the inquisitorial eye of the naked bulb, all space is immediately visible, designed for grave tasks that require utter concentration, dispassionate examination, or rigorous investigation. The house of a shy aunt and uncle, the glare from the fluorescent strip-lights is such that it precludes any unduly intimate contact; should they wish, from time to time, to scratch each other's backs, they have to shut themselves away in a dark nook. Thoughtfully positioned lamps, on the other hand, cast delicate pools of light, affording the apartment a chance to breathe; objects beyond their ambit—the sofa, the volumes on the bookshelves—can breathe freely; in the shadowy space between two pools of light, an enticing after-hours bar slides into the living room.

A solar eclipse quiets the commotion of the day as it does the gaze of all those who witness it. Faced with this cosmic event, people suddenly inhabit the world less arrogantly, with a greater sense of humility and decency as though they have stumbled on some hidden truth, some secret memory. A power failure which plunges a restaurant into darkness so that diners must finish their meal by candlelight fills the room with the echoes of a gentle, unexpected world. This sudden darkness, like the eclipse, is something they have secretly been waiting for, so that it might awaken the better part of their nature, make them feel at peace with themselves.

Others, of course, make the most of the darkness and we arrive home after dinner to discover we have been burgled. We finally manage to get to sleep only to wake in the middle of the night with a start and rush to the wardrobe to make sure the burglars have not stolen a particular jacket or suit. As we mount a silent guard over the wardrobe and, taking out each article of clothing, letting our fingertips roam across the infinite greys, we sink into unsuspected depths; our meticulous thumbing of the wools and tweeds is suddenly our one task, our true vocation.

The light distilled in the flame of a match fleetingly illuminates the face of a stranger smoking and accentuates the solid mass of the surrounding darkness. Within this darkness is hidden the rarest, faintest glimmer, a simple island of light, russet and humid which we constantly seek out in the depths of night-time villages and in the intimate folds of women. Light is the pure coursing of the sun's brilliance offered suddenly as a gift. We need not seek it out, we simply melt eternally into its stream, stepping from our own shadows to find ourselves made whole in the gaze illuminated by the expectations we place in it; we are a part of what we see—face or tree—which returns our gaze, deeper now, made richer by its own brightness. Love: to see and be seen. But there are faces too, with twin tombstone eyes,[2] which have shut us out before they have seen us.

The Prophets and the Fates

Though history is already well advanced, even today, somewhere on the edge of a market or in the half-light of a record shop, there are men who come together in small groups to converse gravely as though their colloquium might save the world. The eldest of the group leads the discussion, alone or with someone with a ready answer; the others listen to the disquisition and now and then breathe new life into it with a question; the ritual of the conversation, the subject of common interest silently unites the men, reinforces their sense of tribal belonging and broadening their knowledge. Already, some of the younger men are preparing their speeches for some future time while others are content to participate in this initiation.

Some distance away—perhaps only on the far side of the stream in the same fishing village—a number of women have gathered in the late afternoon at a bakery or a dry cleaner's. They have nothing to tell each other—they have long known all there is to know, each has her own opinion and all know the same thing; they bring it up only to reconsider it, to laugh about it, giving each other sidelong glances. Above all, they laugh at the Prophets busy setting the world to rights on the other side of the river while the Fates in their shop already know the world and what they can expect of it. They know as much about the world as the Prophets, who, when they have said what they have to say, will be back eating out of their hands. And making promises they cannot keep ... As the rain begins to fall and the half-light of the dry cleaner's turns to twilight, somewhere behind the women in the depths of the shop, darkness yawns like a tomb. One after another the Prophets come scurrying, while from among the most seductive Fates, soon to be widowed, an austere man hidden within them inexorably emerges.

(We will go home, but not without some trepidation; before we go we linger for a while in a small café with or without our partners-in-crime. We know that women are insatiable, we know that whatever we give them will never be enough; we know that in the depths of their most intimate crevice yawns a chasm which is not a part of them, but some stranger they are sheltering. They allow us our moments of triumph, sometimes go so far as to congratulate us, but they never cease to crave more. We can go back to them in the evenings or go elsewhere; leave the cares of the home to them or help them, allow ourselves to be cosseted or brave the dangers of the world for them. They never cease to wait for their own arrival, just as they await the arrival of that other man destined to share their lives in our stead and who has been delayed somewhere. And so we tell ourselves that this might be enough, that we have carried off our solo, that we have made the trombone proudly yowl, the hammer discreetly chime, all that remains is for us to leave the stage like those who came before us. And to finally free ourselves from the fear to which the Fates abandoned us, and from the constant censure their eyes turn on us and on the Cosmos.)

The Unknown Woman

For Milan Kundera

A YOUNG GIRL ON A TRAIN, SITTING OPPOSITE, or on a plane sometimes, a little further off, so beautiful that we allow our gaze to circle back to her, snuggles all the more closely against the man next to her, hugs him, presses herself against him to prove that she belongs to him. As she turns her back on us, her blouse rucked up to reveal—almost to offer us—her naked body. And she knows all too well, knows better than we, that this enticing glimpse of flesh belongs to no one, not even to herself; that with its silent yet unyielding radiance, blinding in spite of itself, it is no more than a strip of *no man's land*.[3]

When, in the night, in the apartment upstairs or the one across the hall, an unknown woman howls beneath the body of an unknown man, she is intentionally flaunting her pleasure, making us jealous, but in that moment she is also offering herself to us. The cry that rends the silence makes the encircling night visible like a continuum of which we are a part, in which we too make love as in a crowded dormitory. The cry, apparently intended for her lover, slips his embrace to turn inexorably toward us—or rather, toward no one, since it is no more intended for us than for her lover but only for the omnipresent cosmos. Even the great stars of the silver screen, when looking up towards the camera, eyes brimming with tears, are not looking at the audience any more than they are looking at their co-star; they are trying to beguile the cosmos itself. The eyes which gaze deeply into ours, like the cries of women, are indirect, forever oblique and menacing.

We repay them in kind; when Keaton[4] aims resolutely at a target in a shooting gallery only to hit the one on the right, it is an honest portrayal of us and of our questionable conquests.

The Leave-taking

As she leaves the party to go home to bed, and as she sways still, catching her breath on the threshold a little, neither beautiful nor plain, simply "Lilian" (we call out after her), belonging without belonging to herself—every man present attempts to picture her panties, her removing her panties, what remains after she takes them off. And afterwards? There is no afterwards; she leaves and each man, as best he can, attempts to picture her underwear, the removal, what remains.

The Cunt

For John and Jitka Bok

IN SPITE OF ITS APPARENT OFFENSIVENESS, there is no better word. In contrast to the clinical 'sex' or the seductive 'pussy', 'cunt' definitively describes the fascinating thing—including its hidden bone—just as it complements its subject: the brusque tension it introduces into the world. It thus evokes even the appalling starkness of a buttoned dress under which the thing encourages us to crudely despoil it, just like the hardness that lurks behind even the gentlest desires: the longing for a brutal fuck, slamming against the wardrobe, right here, standing up, at the lowest ebb of night or on some arid day. The word seems to hesitate between the concrete and the abstract, now fingering the mass, the curve of the thing, now turning towards its distant fantasy. The thing is judicious, for years it is no more than a vague intimation, a target and a question mark between two thighs out of reach; then, suddenly, as an unknown figure comes towards us along a street in springtime, it is suddenly a promontory caressed by the folds of a skirt. The skirt and the underwear beneath, touching then not touching, lined with hair, feeling as it grows damp, then open and begin the examination, enter, follow the trail, seek out the depths. The cunt is a quest, it is that which lies before us waiting to be found, to be discovered, to be conquered, deeper in yourself and in the night, in the secret depths of the thicket, of the poem.

The Onion and the Rose

THE ONION AND THE ROSE, by their distant kinship, are quietly complicit—their similarities and dissimilarities extend as far as the eye can see—each illuminating the other, revealing its meaning. The rose, with its skilfully folding scented velvets and the rift of night at its centre, is both a labyrinth and a symbol of femininity, of its charms, its hidden trap and its secret—impregnable—abyss. The pungent onion, the poor man's rose, is the maze of the everyday peregrinations, it is secrecy brought back to necessity, essential to survival; whereas learning how to smell the rose, how to fathom it represents an arduous poetic task for all existence, the initiatory rite in the case of the onion consists simply of appropriating and mastering one of the common methods of peeling and cutting it. True, from this simple task, one acquires something of the patience and the wisdom necessary to the pursuit of greater pleasures; first crying as you slice the onion, only then browning it in the frying pan, adding a tender piece of red meat—already covering it with caresses—and slowly reaching paradise as the meat slowly surrenders, giving off its aroma.

Mid-way between the onion and the rose is the cabbage, still purely practical and yet, in cross-section, it inexorably draws us in with the curves of its astounding and feminine folds. As to the singular thing—and image—of the mystery that is the egg, it is surprising and poignant not least because of the efforts of the man who, with an eternally childlike artfulness, stubbornly tries to make it disappear in his magician's hat.

You

Compared to the more aggressive but primal 'fuck you' and the French *'va te faire foutre'*, the Czech *'Vyliz si prdel'*—'go lick your arse'—is not only more subtle, it condemns the interlocutor to a more humiliating act. Tongues buried in their own cracks, the morons gutter out like damp squibs in the park, as along the outskirts of a paradise newly unsullied—at least for the time it takes to hurl insults at them.

Night

1

NIGHT IS COME, its scope, its depth unknowable. What happenings does it hide? Cars crisscross a darkened square with the drone of distant planets, a path shudders beneath the hurried footsteps of prey and, moments later, those of predator. Behind their darkened windows, men stand frozen as around them objects come to life, in the darkness women become widows, become lustful, somewhere deep in the darkness, our house disintegrates into rubble. In the dead of night is a mountain lake and the roar of blood in the temples of the observer standing on its shore. The night-time forest affords shelter to black strawberries; in the bedroom, the piece of furniture we will trip over in the morning lies in wait next to a cradle filled with darkness. Night haunts the night, in the depths of its being it knows everything and nothing of itself, on the edge of night, loud-mouthed fools insist on singing their own praises.

2

We get up in the middle of the night, though we are not truly awake, we are, rather, a wisp of darkness and motion; only from a distance, with eyes half-closed, can we see the darkness slide over itself in slow waves while in the kitchen, a glass of water—a luminous thread of the present cutting across the flow of time—

trickles into our entrails. We are and are not here, merely a shape, a movement of a legend beyond memory, the cool trickle of the water roots us so clearly in the moment that from this point, as from some gloomy airport, everything is equidistant—the beginnings of History and all possible machinations and their outcomes. In the bathroom, the white mass of the bath surges out of the darkness like a lofty iceberg; the woman next to whom we lie down again to sleep is still alive and breathes in the midst of History, perhaps for us.

The Jerusalem artichoke

G OING TO THE KITCHEN, seeing the Jerusalem artichoke then silently going back to bed.

Connected, Disconnected

For Vlasta

E VERY SLEEPWALKER, wrapped up in himself, in meadows, on distant rooftops, is alone and yet each is connected to every other; moonlight binds them with a powerful bond and melds them into the warp and weft of a single tremulous backcloth. In spite of their garrulous fury, men in the streets jabbering into their mobile phones are disconnected from everyone and everything, even from themselves; moreover they disconnect the innocent bystanders with whom they mingle. Even sleepwalkers with mobile phones do not reconnect to one another until the moon cuts short the call.

Dusk

THE ARRIVAL OF DUSK fleetingly lays all things bare but it also makes things clear—beginning with the transience of day; in this sense it is more real than the night which romantically insinuates that its darkness hides the key to all our desires. Enclosed within this pool of shadow, those who have spent the day floating hazily in space now find themselves grown solid, their outlines growing more distinct somewhere in the suburbs; rooted to the kerb or to a lamppost as though a part of it, forming with the surrounding objects fleeting yet sharply-defined images which, perhaps, are also signs. Together, they even form unexpected unions. A street reader's newspaper and the bare calf in a shop doorway have been welded into a single white knot, a group of people chatting on the corner have formed a pallid monument; one need only look in their direction to know which way to go. Only on the cusp of Saturday afternoon, sometimes, might a cool body appear so sharply defined beneath the layers of a taffeta dress tried on before the ball that night … Even she whom we barely glimpsed in daylight in the metro now at dusk offers herself to us, more precisely delineated, we can see the mourning skirt that we take off her as clearly as the grey wall against which we press her body. The man who walked out to the gate of his villa as the day drew to a close still stands there, sharing this makeshift *parloir* with the friend on the far side of the gate. Each through the other greets the world—he who stepped out of his house as much as he who rang the doorbell—each is both prisoner and messenger from afar; each, at this twilight hour is part dog, part wolf.[5] Night finally falls and the friends go their separate ways and in the darkness the gate is no more than a metal grill growing cold.

Attacking

IT IS NOT ENOUGH that we get up, cross the threshold, step out into the day and in it open strange and unfamiliar doors; somewhere in the depths of the day, we are called on to perform a task, do a job, perform a solo, stand guard, get our hair cut, go to the doctor for a check-up. Sometimes, without realising, barely have we stepped out into the street when some distant goal, some person, rears up ahead, bearing down on us—to which every step brings us closer. Stepping inside a rundown barber shop, what comes to greet us is something more than our reflection in the tarnished mirror. The footsteps of the last gunman, as he steps into the vanquished city to end a war, stirs one last thunderous blast from the ruins; sometimes an ageing composer is flushed from his hiding place, providing our sniper with one last target.

The war did not end when the Jews in Theresienstadt concentration camp discovered that the wall in the Kleine Festung that they spent their days building was intended to seal off the courtyard so they could be drowned inside it: and so they left an inconspicuous gap in the wall, and every day, always with some new excuse, they came back to ensure it was open. Every morning as they set to work, the gap in the far wall—at once a back door and a mutinous opening into the future—greeted them with a smile. A gap waits for us, too—be it only some humble gap we open up by the preparations we make for the attack, by setting out our tools, our paperwork or our drums and cymbals and inspecting them, a first cigarette dangling from our lips. It is a task we would be wise not to shirk; the attentiveness with which we open the door to the doctor's surgery as he appears at the door down the hall—already asking us what the trouble is—may significantly influence his diagnosis.

But it is not simply about us, nor the welcome we prepare for ourselves by the manner in which we enter into the world; our cautious tread as we step into the forest puffs up with pride the *cèpes* that stand, deep within, on the edge of a clearing we will never reach. In fact, it is possible that our step into the forest is simply an echo of the mushrooms' resolute surging above the mosses; for his part, the doctor may have chosen us just as we chose him, summoning us to his surgery as a mirror image, a necessary counterpart to himself. The drummer in the band we came to hear, glancing towards us from the far end of the hall as we step over the threshold, has his sights on some distant target far above our heads, his glance ricochets all the way to the random traffic on the ring road, the brush on the snare drum stirring up the anonymous rustle of leaves eddying in suburban gardens. Then, as we turn our backs on him to leave, nothing is truly closed; even before we shut the door behind us, someone hurries to open the fridge behind the bar, unleashing a beam of light into the darkness like some last-minute attempt to be a part of our lives.

The Wind

A HIGH WIND WARNING SOUNDS LIKE the first line of a new chapter bringing us back to life, shivering slightly, like a vast *roman fleuve* thundering towards the next episode; we all but find ourselves swallowed up by History again. A solitary gust of wind is enough to unlock the day, to comb the leaves and the bushes, to rise and to let us hear the bass notes that are the secret accompaniment to life itself. Sometimes a gust of wind marks out the day by some remarkable event: a motorway pile-up, an unexpectedly lucky throw of the dice; a gentleman's hat is whipped away, a dog watches dumbfounded as the newspaper rears up, a skirt pressed tight against the woman is suddenly grey to its very core.

Darkness and Twilight

DEEP SHADOW OR NIGHT'S DARKNESS conceals objects leaving us to intuit their shape, their size, to read from their outlines, from the faint light they emit the heft of an anvil, the softness of a shoulder, the favours or the dangers of flesh. Only the twilight makes it possible to see them as they truly are, only the half-light reveals, accentuates the subtle nuances of skin or of a gleaming dressmaker's dummy. Darkness is sensual, twilight is metaphysical, initiatory; we aim for the darkness between a pair of thighs, but search for it in the half-light.

Twilight is to night as grey is to black; we stumble into black as we might a piece of furniture in a darkened hallway, but we linger in the grey, it is the colour of the unhurried understanding of objects, of the persistence of things. All the world's riches are in the gradations of grey of black-and-white photographs, the vanished summer preserved within their ashes. Grey immediately signals a truce, it appeases conflict, mutes the insistent, overweening arrogance of the world and those who inhabit it. As they move through the grey day, timorously hugging the walls, passing pedestrians in raincoats melt almost completely into the background, become almost a part of History, faithfully following its course. The same History of which, long ago, the first motorcyclists were a part, when they were merely delicate shadows on the windy boulevards, their scarves discreetly floating. Grey days make our own perceptions less insistent, focussing them on the faint quivering of a single twig, honing them until they finally dissolve into the restful silence of sensation.

Grey is unquestionably something more than greyness, the colour of monotony and everyday tedium—though our sense of grey contributes to our experience of these things, of the listless hours and our struggle to contend with them. In other forms, tones of grey make up a rich and varied spectrum, the sombre grey of the cemetery, the solid grey of stone, the flaking grey of slate, the sly grey of a pigeon, the noble grey of a pearl, rain-grey, railway station grey, suburban grey. The white which grey both foretells and forestalls—just as it does black—illuminates it from within, sounding its depths to the hidden glimmer of bone grey beneath the ashes. The vulgar brilliant white of newly fallen snow is as unrelated to grey—and to its metaphysic—as deepest black; the natural luminosity of grey glistens in the mother-of-pearl façades of buildings as they appear in the first light of morning, like still waters, their surface rippled only by the soundless sighs from chinks in the stone.

There are laconic greys and languid greys, elegant greys and greys which seem regretful somehow, as though apologising for themselves; apologising perhaps for their elegance. No grey, however, is insistent: while black clothes underscore the solemnity of mourning, grey maintains a respectful distance. For this same reason, of the two flowers—twin trophies—most highly prized, the grey rose is prized above the black, precisely for the additional quality which is its slight reserve. Those women who pique our desire when dressed in black, only become our true loves, our allies against the day's intemperance when dressed in grey. Men in black summon us to deliver curt judgements; men in grey spend hours with us conversing about the way of the world. The man with the grey face is a messenger whose importance is all the greater for the fact that, stepping from the crowd, he lifts his face to meet us with all the enthusiasm of a humble tradesman, a postman or a meter reader. The postman, of course, delivers his most profound message to us only after his shift has ended, when standing at the bar drinking with the local butcher, the serene grey of his uniform—so different from the sombre uniform of policemen—melts into the half-light of the café, his simple presence communicating to all those present a remarkable piece of news of which he himself is ignorant.

The Hotel

For Michal Ajvaz

A HOTEL ROOM IS a fiction, a stage set in which we are content to make believe we live; but it also offers us undreamt-of possibilities, separates our actions, our performance from the network of necessity, affording them a wider scope. A night spent in a hotel, even with a familiar partner, takes on a fresh, almost forbidden, sense. We are touched, even excited when, in the stage set that is a hotel, we discover some genuinely domestic detail: it may be no more than the panes of coloured glass in the kitchen door to which the owner retreats like a welcome refuge, it may be an easel with a half-finished painting abandoned confidently beside our bed. Italian hoteliers, aware of our weakness for such juxtapositions, discreetly enhance their hotel rooms with their own furniture: a rustic armoire or an antique candlestick.

Even when we travel alone, from the moment we step through the door, a hotel room can afford a glimpse of some utterly unfamiliar life—or some unsuspected part of our own—and a set in which to live out at least some fragment of that life. Should we book a whole suite, a whole series of lives appear before us; the bed in the dark room at the end of the corridor seems to have been especially conceived so that, at night, we can run our fingers through the wings of some mysterious angel, while the sofa in a small alcove lit by a steep skylight offers a place where the pale radiance of our afternoon naps can shine forth as never before.

Home from our travels, we are often surprised by our own apartment, where we suddenly discover hidden nooks and crannies; gaze into the mysterious depths of some familiar nook, peer behind the bed, the bath, between the fault-lines of the books on the shelves, our gaze unveiling the successive layers of these hidden alcoves it reveals, here in our own home, the unsuspected flipside of a stage set. If we ourselves cannot live behind the scenes, a chorus of humble tailors, pale swimming instructors, listless lions—perhaps even gentle sleepwalkers—step unseen from the wings, their hushed, complicit breath attending us during our stay here.

Rain

Whenever rain lingers awhile—even a soft rain—it is welcome, because it disturbs the course of the day and veils the world from itself. It brings to the day something of night's darkness by giving it a greater depth, putting it out of play in a way, the better to breathe from within. It also reverberates within itself for as far as the eye can see; the austere perpendicularity of its curtains does not prevent the rain from sending them floating off in all directions, scattering them with the intricacy of a baroque fugue, while elsewhere—out towards the horizon and in its own hidden centre—it opens up new spaces. Nameless courtyards, gardens, niches, ramshackle rooftop footbridges, the paths around the park, ordinarily lost in oblivion, rise beneath the raindrops to the surface and play an important part in this cosmic event, sending it back echoes of itself; they are not alone in this—rain also carves out new spaces within space itself, brings to light a second landscape behind the first and reveals, between the raindrops, vast warehouses and hangars filled with sacks, with leaking containers, with pulleys and winches eaten away with rust. Rain can afford us a glimpse of the hidden reserves of our apartment where sometimes, in addition to the unfamiliar nooks and cupboards, the rain's reverberations can lead us to discover a whole storeroom we never knew existed. This in-depth work does not mean that it neglects the surface aspect of things, of the world, as we see it every day; on the contrary, it washes their nakedness with such gentle care that the true meaning of objects is restored. The worn surface of objects reveals their inner glow, just as the pattering of the raindrops reconciles speech and simple murmurs, bringing to the meaning of words their possible ambiguity. Similarly, rain connects the surface and the depths; as the waves lift undersea chasms towards the heavens, elsewhere, the raindrops pattering on a table make the plain wood shine gloriously, flat and smooth forever.

Though it opens up new spaces to us, the rain is merely a fleeting guest, which washes us and washes us away in turn. If the clatter of the raindrops that fill the streets makes the rain seem more akin to cinema than dreaming is, it is because rain strips film down to its essentials: a simple flickering of light and shadow that fades from the screen as soon as they have appeared. In this, the rain that falls at dead of night is particularly eloquent—sounding its own depths, sending back nothing but echoes of the desolate lateness of the hour—it merges as never before into the boundless search for a 'sense of self'. The sudden noises, sudden echoes which here and there it taps out on a piece of corrugated iron, on a discarded bottle, bring to life objects that are nothing more than ghosts which conjure the subtle forms and colours of this vacant scene. The rain-sodden shapes we fleetingly imagine roaming the outskirts of the city are the last heroes, the patter of the rain sufficient to applaud them for us. True, certain passers-by, sombre bureaucrats of the rain, have been carrying the weight of it in their bodies, in their faces since the afternoon, sometimes accompanied by a sad dog.

Others appeared briefly before the camera in the dying day just as the rain began to threaten and, distracted from their serious tasks, rushed to close a casement window, looking up towards the lowering sky. When, as we are out walking, rain begins to murmur around us, it spurs us towards some tranquil boarding house at the heart of the world—while somewhere on the edge, the raindrops measure space as they splatter against an anvil we have left outside.

Familiarity

For Jiří Fiala

THE RAIN WHICH CATCHES US UNAWARES outside a run-down café, urging us inside, makes it possible for us to inhabit the premises for a moment, or even to wait out the apocalypse. And yet the café we regularly go to is simply the one where, one morning, we sip a glass of white wine next to the policeman on his way to the station, who has popped in to pick up the helmet he left there the night before.

Blots and Off-cuts

For Roman Erben

IN OUR CHILDHOOD, we were taught to pour molten lead into cold water and take it out, transformed now into bizarre concretions; adults would claim to see in these shapes men, animals, objects, whole scenes, perhaps even images of events yet to come. We humoured them, but kept our counsel; though we also found these solid shapes intriguing it was rather as strange symbols, characters from some mysterious alphabet. We found the same intriguing shapes in spatters of blood or quicklime, in pools of hardened sealing wax, in the ink blots we doodled on the pages in our copybook in spite of the scolding it earned us. Each ambiguous blot was a sign, one made all the more pressing since it combined the legibility of a figure with the opacity of a substance; vacillating between the abstraction of a letter and the solidity of an object, while melting both—as though to mutually reinforce the presence of each—into a single symbol: a letter with the insistent materiality of a squashed dog. The enigma we sensed in these blots was to haunt us forever; even now we long to discover the secrets we glimpsed within them.

When we were taken to the tailor's and he began to dance for us, scissors clacking, tape measure snapping, swathing us in a length of fabric on which he would trace intricate chalk patterns—the way he looked after us commended us to a life of adventure, of travel to foreign lands; the tide of cloth that swelled about us, as about some dumbfounded buoy, foreshadowed the ocean rippled by breezes as far as the distant horizon and the yacht on which we would sail across it, accompanied by ladies with pale skirts. We had only to glance down at the off-cuts scattered over the table in the living room, feel the fabric scraps that the tailor gave us to examine, and we were ready to set sail for far-flung cities, to see lightning flash unexpectedly above the port, the houses.

When we finally draw alongside, we go ashore to explore the cities, scour the suburbs in a meticulous search to discover the city's secret, the reason why we have come here. We overlook nothing, neither the crowd suddenly gathering on a public square in the centre nor a lighted dormer window which looks down upon the square at night; the secret may be waiting for us anywhere. And yet we search in ever decreasing circles until finally a shop window, appearing silently before us in the depths of the afternoon, makes us realise we need look no further: we have come to the city to see the old tailor—now almost the last of his kind in the world—who, behind the picture window, leans over the great tailor's goose; we have come simply to pay him a visit and to rummage through the off-cuts in the half-light of the shop as outside the rain begins to fall.

To live: to wander far from the original tailor, look questioningly at the sky as it clouds over while still attempting to decipher the message in the blots and the spatters by the roadside. And also, of course, while listening attentively to the drummers and the doors they open with every crash, to hear their tattoo measure the surrounding space in our stead, like the space inside an unfamiliar house abandoned to the breeze.

The Curve

For Michel Deguy

A BREAK IN THE MONOTONOUS STRETCH OF ROAD; only a curve gives meaning to the journey and transforms it into a joy. It is hardly surprising that a train, as it rounds a curve, lets out a whistle and blows a proud plume of smoke towards the heavens, while over the towering reef that is New York, city of cities, looms the secret affront that it towers over a rigid checkerboard without a single curve. A curve is a necessary extravagance which alone can ease our prosaic sojourn in this world, turning our journey into a dance. Even the pleasures of love are in its meanders—without which it would be no more than the simple shunting of a piston—the loops and leashes of seduction, a fluttering skirt, a glove, a hat gracefully removed, gentle detours by the curve of a shoulder or the delicate hollow of the elbow. The bend. A curve allows us to dally awhile among transitory things, to let our eye linger on the gleam of a shard of glass and the paleness of a bush by the roadside as it slides along the horizon.

To the enemy we circle during our sorties, we pay a distant homage; a bend in a night-time landscape where we are caught unawares by a storm is a whole world; the combine harvester in the field, lit by a flash of lightning from behind, looms over the scene like a sleeping god. By day, a bend in the road shimmers before our eyes like a heat haze, the better to make us feel its caress as it turns us like a page and sets us down again in the landscape like some lost fragment of itself. We have no other goal than a successfully circumnavigated bend—and in doing so, once again circumvent our own end—no other triumph than the smile that it resembles, than the smile it instinctively brings to our lips. If we could but live our lives in curves, it is obvious we would be here forever.

Graze

It sometimes happens that, as we round a bend, we graze the barrier; our forward momentum is not fatally jeopardised, in fact it is enlivened. This fleeting contact with the barrier reminds us that it is there, our near miss adds drama to the corner, but it also stirs an echo in which we suddenly *hear* ourselves take the bend, making us more aware of our own breathing and that of the whole world. Our encounter with the barrier differs depending on the nature of the contact, on whether we merely graze it or crash into it. To graze your shoulder with my tongue, then draw away a long gossamer thread in the clear September light, towards your armpit, towards the hard shoulder of damp sand, tracing the curve into its salty depths. Mid-way between grazing and crashing, when we scrape along a length of the barrier, it can prove fatal or glorious, it may end in disaster or deliverance. As he plays, Roy Haynes[6] skims the edge of the drum or the cymbal like the circumference of eternity, he is a flint from which eternity draws fresh sparks, sketching out the arc of its arena more vividly.

Conquest

For Gianfranco Sanguinetti

TO ELICIT A GLOW FROM A DESERTED BEND, from the indifferent whiteness of a page, to penetrate night's darkness to the small damp flame within; perhaps merely to tease a flame from a match. To fashion a solo from the simple decision to play, or to merely make the instrument sound. The latter may earn you a day's pay, the former in addition, elicits a distant mournful wail. One day, a Lothario, besotted with a young English girl who has never seen Venice, asks her to go on a dull business trip with him, intending—though he does not tell her this—to take her to the Serenissima. On the train, he discreetly draws the curtains and so hides the view of the *laguna*. When she steps out of the railway station and realises where she is, the girl stands rooted to the spot, staring at the palazzo across the canal and her whole body begins to silently tremble. She has been conquered.

By Hand

To initiate an amorous offensive with the hand is tantamount to an ambush; unlike a simple kiss, which falls within the scope of conventional warfare, a hand placed suddenly on a thigh has the precision of a *coup de grâce*, and sunders time itself: the moment before belongs to the past, the hand slipped onto the thigh is the dawn of a new era. To slip that same hand directly between the thighs is—for all its literalness—a more decisive gesture still; whereas a sensitive Moravian poet was wont to gaze nostalgically at the night sky above the treetops, whose branches—he claimed—sound the night's depths in our absence, this frontal attack shakes the treetops and sometimes reveals a secret rigging behind the leaves. But we are not common robbers, our hand does not seek to paw a woman's crevices, her curves out of mere lust; our attack is also—is first and foremost—a defence against the onslaught of her beauty, her charms; the hand that now assails her is attempting a counter-attack.

When we take a woman's hand, we yearn not for her body, but for what that body conceals; the sudden urge to touch her has all the pathos of a pact in which we strive to bring together the loneliness and the finiteness of two individuals against the world's inhumanity, the emptiness of the cosmos. The boundary between a lover's gesture and one that is simply human is ambiguous, the gestures overlap, nor is it always clear, like the famous chicken and her egg, which comes first. In the thigh so suddenly molested lurks the thrum of loneliness and the possible coming together of the twin nakedness of two *existences*; simply to reach out a hand to the individual in the other body is exciting, it fires our desire for that body. Unless perhaps the true meaning of desire is to allow us, through the aura of beauty another's body confers on us, to assume responsibility for our own body, the better to inhabit our own skin. But, no one, as you say, can save us.

Grown-Ups

For my mother

WHEN THE GROWN-UPS HAD GUESTS, they used to persuade us to go to bed or into the next room; we pretended to do as we were told, but instead of going to sleep, we would come back and press our ear to the door and, through the shudders of the door and the chinks of light, drink in every word, every voice, every chink of glass like some message filled with meaning. We were eager to know what lay in store for us; in our absence, grown-ups busied themselves with the world, with the life they were preparing for us, with some strange game of which one day we would be a part. A game so mysterious, so important that it seemed beyond even their comprehension, as though the grown-ups had not quite mastered the rules. In the mirror, we might glimpse a decisive moment as mother brought her hand up to her necklace and furtively glanced over her shoulder at one of father's tennis partners. Perhaps in their clamour, the grown-ups did not hear the engines of the ship on the far side of the door which was already carrying them farther and farther away.

Years later, we come home from our own parties, not quite understanding how we came to be there—it is not that we do not make the effort, we work at it enthusiastically, sometimes still painstakingly trying to piece together how the party went and what happened the next morning. One evening, after dinner, as we step from the kitchen back into our own living room, we are surprised to find the familiar grown-up world, that warm nest with its mingled scents of smoke, of *hors d'oeuvres* and wine, that once upon a time we could smell from the other side of the door. But the grown-ups are gone now, and so are we.

The Party

For Miloš (and for Prokop)

Last night's party was a success, a friend's astonishing midnight dance made us laugh, by the window, another friend whispered something to us that seemed like a fundamental truth. For our part, sadly, we came up with no brilliant insights and were painfully inept in our dancing. As a result we are therefore all the more grateful to our friends, something we tell them affectionately as we chat about the party. The dancer remembers nothing about his party piece except for the ringing slap his partner gave him, but he talks excitedly about our pale elegance as we danced the tango while the friend we chatted to by the window thanks us for pointing out to him some remarkable reveller passing outside. It remains to be seen which of us was at the *right* party.

The Arena

For Jiří Pavel (and for Prokop)

THE EXPANSE OF GRASS circumscribed by the cycle track, the quadrangle bounded by colonnades and cloisters breathing silently at the heart of a monastery, the ellipse of a lake: so many arenas offering spaces from which we might conquer the world from within. There is no need to leave for a crusade; we need only focus on the centre of the scene, as ambiguous as it appears to be accessible, which seems within our grasp yet still eludes us; the more we approach, the more it retreats, forcing us to bring a heightened attention to bear on what is before us and what is within us. In this sense, the arena is a symbol of an inner infinity, while all around as night falls the surrounding cosmos diminishes—only a passing stranger opens up the night as he walks by the arena, grazing the ellipse in passing like a tangent. With the dishes cleared away, the table now presents another arena before which we linger, alone; but through the ashtray—a miniature cloister—in the centre, we transform this solitude into dialogue merely by staring at the cigarette butt—or simply at the ashes—inside. As we clean the ashtray before we go to bed, with a serviette or the cork of an empty bottle, we glimpse the dawn breaking in the distance.

Years ago, in our house in the country, the hum of anticipation before a party and our longing to understand the ways of the world would send us rushing with our friends up into the attic—which was to us a mysterious world filled with adventure. In an old trunk, beside the postcards from exotic places, the explorer's clothes lay in wait. Here in the attic we would pose as globe-trotting adventurers for some girl we fancied, a girl we persuade to step out onto the roof with us. There, ready to storm the summit; we turn to one another, our eyes ablaze, only to find the same bewilderment. And we go on babbling, talking feverishly about the world, about ourselves, in spite of the silence which sweeps through us. We even find some common ground, but the experiment is one we are reluctant to repeat. We feel as alone together as we do when, each in our own bumper car, we weave between the other cars, a crest of sparks crackling above our heads; or when playing hide-and-seek we find a hiding place where we are surrounded by inanimate objects, only to emerge, one after another, each carrying the hidden secret in our eyes, resurfacing little by little.

In this same way, we share our sojourn in the world when we glance towards the ashtray, towards the centre of the room; we need only an adjoining room in which it is constantly raining so that together we can listen to the patter of the raindrops, so that we can share a home with our companions. Some of them secretly search to see whether we are not hiding the room somewhere, or eavesdrop on our silent bedroom. Though they may not live in the same house, we recognise in them our true partners-in-crime.

Elsewhere

For Martin Pluháček

EVEN IN THE COURSE of a thoroughly enjoyable evening with friends in a *brasserie*, the assembled company may suddenly feel the urge to go elsewhere, to move on to some other establishment; sometimes barely have you arrived and settled in when you find yourself wondering where you might go *afterwards*. Do we really want to be here in this *brasserie*, would we not rather go home to bed, sinking back into half-light, into ourselves, into the depths of the inclement winter, sulking alone, bored, every man for himself, far from *brasserie* and friends? Perhaps we are afraid that from now on we will exchange only bewildered looks as we did in the attic years ago. Or perhaps we would like to open a little café with our friends, a grotto just for us, perhaps even take them home and make our home the locus of all our get-togethers. Perhaps we wish we could take the others elsewhere, beyond the apartment, to some secret depths within ourselves, to long ago when friends were merely longed-for shadows, projected onto the bare walls of our cave. As if, in the half-light of a platonic *brasserie*, the circles could grow both narrower and wider …

The Nobody Moment

THERE COMES A MOMENT, after we have finished eating with a friend, when there are only a few last drops to be wrung from the bottle; yet only now do we really feel at ease, both in the restaurant itself as in our conversation. The train hurtles at full speed, sleepers groan beneath the weight of our conversation; to add to the clatter, we order two more glasses of brandy. But no sooner do they arrive than someone cuts the throttle, the brakes squeal: it is closing time—if we are to continue our journey we must go elsewhere.

The neighbourhood is deserted, plunged into darkness and a light drizzle has begun to fall. Fortunately, around the corner we stumble on one of those slightly surreal last-chance oases you find in urban deserts unsure of their status, timidly boastful against a backdrop of dreary provincialism. The soft pink neon and the familiar name (*Chez Emilie?*) marks the place out as midway between a bar and a sort of local club frequented by dog breeders or would-be Buddhist bridge players; in the cellar at the bottom of the steep flight of stairs the narrow booths are empty but for a silent hulking man in a tracksuit or a couple of phoney customers hiding from the parents—from secret partners—from the imposing figure of the masseuse whose maternal eye keeps watch over the premises. We order a snifter of brandy and continue on our journey, only to suddenly grind to a halt once more; there is only time now for one for the road. They too arrive, this time it really is the last; but we can linger over them awhile, the masseuse has cashed up, her cashbox closing with a clack, but still the waiting room of the cellar is open to us.

We drain our glasses, we have said all we had to say, we can hear only the dying echoes of our conversation and the nocturnal stillness of this bar where we have washed up, we feel oddly moved by the emptiness of the booths all around us, the bare, hard wood of the partitions staunches the waves of music spilling from a radio in the lobby where the masseuse has definitively retreated with the parents. A nobody moment, the most obvious, the most colossal secret we will take away from the evening.

The Gents

IN THE GENTS WE LEARN TO SHOW A CERTAIN consideration to others and to ourselves; especially when we suddenly find ourselves sharing the silence and the intimacy of *brasserie* toilets with another customer, whether someone from our own table or some stranger drinking at the other end of the bar. It is situation shrewdly summed up by the old joke in which a nervous man in the gents casually remarks to the stranger next to him: "How come you seem to be making so much noise? I can hardly hear myself pissing?" and the other man replies: "That's because you're pissing on my coat!" The man's good-natured but embarrassed reply says all there is to say about the embarrassment two men feel standing in front of a urinal, holding their breath, attentively staring at the tiles directly in front of them in the trickling silence. Finding yourself in this delicate situation with a friend gives rise to very different conversations to those you might have at the table with the rest of the group; sometimes it may prompt shared confidences, unexpected insights; the—unwritten—record of lavatorial conversations is filled with momentous words forever lost to posterity. Consequently, we leave the Gents not simply relieved but head back to our table like a scouting patrol bringing back new information, a new perspective on the world, sometimes even a new partner-in-crime.

The Gents also offers an arena in which rival males may mutually compare themselves. We glance surreptitiously toward our neighbour to measure his good fortune, his intimate reserves, to glimpse an alien destiny, gauge its length; sometimes—with a sense of relief—we glimpse the extent of his misfortune. When a vagrant steps up beside us at the urinal in a run-down railway station in Barcelona, and with a sly glance, we surprise him hard at work, furtively but furiously stroking his swelling purple glans, we penetrate more deeply the secret spaces of the city.

The Bath

Even before we step inside, the dazzling polished whiteness of the bathroom appears as a heaven; its cold, stark, Swiss functionality recalls a mausoleum or a dull Sunday spent at home; we would prefer to linger in the muted murky hell of dark-panelled rooms festooned with cushions, tapestries and accumulated dust. But the bathroom affords its own attractions; aside from the remorseless shower it offers the welcoming bath into which we can already feel ourselves slip as into bed. But the bath is both a refuge and a prison, even a trap. As children, it was here that we felt most pampered, most closely watched; even Charlie Chaplin,[7] when he falls asleep in the bath after a night's drinking, is both revelling in the world of which he is master and anticipating the nightmarish scene in a later film[8] where he wakes up, up to his neck in water in a waterlogged bunk in the flooded trench. Even in a western, when the hero affords himself the luxury of a bath in a local hotel, he cannot completely relax; he must be careful not to get so comfortable in the bath that he can't draw his Colt and fire at the bad guy who hoped to surprise him.

In a bath, we feel too exposed to truly relax and enjoy a long soak; it is pointless to invite a lady friend to join us—in a bath even the most beautiful body flounders like a tadpole, like a human guinea pig, its proximity is simply that of another victim. Though we may be determined to unwind, to wallow in the bath, after only a few minutes we abandon our attempts to relax and begin to scrub ourselves quickly, obsessively—perhaps we still have time to get out of the bath before a killer smashes the door in and turns this bath—this bed on which we tryst with our own frailty—into our tomb.

The Shitter

In every bistro, every *brasserie*, there is a shitter; he sits enthroned behind a locked door and strains; in vain people try the handle, gently at first, then more insistently. Perhaps the door is simply stuck, perhaps whoever is inside has fallen asleep; then the shitter lets out a groan and goes on straining. He strains till it brings tears to his eyes, it is all he can do—he cannot hear, cannot see, probably cannot drink, cannot eat—it is as though this were the one thing he knows how to do: sitting and straining. For our part, we wait, sipping our drink; in spirit we linger with him still, watching as he pushes, flushes, puffs. Finally the door creaks and the shitter returns; we turn, eyes wide, to finally catch a glimpse of him—but it is too late, he has already reverted to being nondescript, unremarkable, barely noticeable as though it were not really him. Has he somehow managed to shit himself out?

Sometimes, we are the shitter; we sit stubbornly, holding the door closed, turning a deaf ear—whoever is knocking can fuck off. We know their sort—they would be only too happy to catch us here unawares; but it won't be so easy, they will have to wait, these prying neighbours, these vindictive women, these outlaws who tried to kill us in the bath. When we return, everyone behaves as though nothing has happened, as though we never left the room—ourselves first and foremost. And yet it is all the more obvious: the premises will never be the same again.

Crossing the Street

At first glance, nothing is more impressive than a public square successfully crossed, and not merely to the inexperienced eye of the novice. Such a crossing is undeniably striking and confers considerable prestige on the pedestrian—especially if, half-way across the square, he should stop and gracefully doff his hat to someone. Even the simple crossing of a street is a difficult task, at least for those not content to simply dash across with an unremarkable glide. The difficulty stems not from the other pedestrians crossing simultaneously, before whom we are eager not to lose face, and who valiantly urge us not to block their path, to leave the way clear for them to pass, or cross with less studied casualness; nor are we daunted by the snarl of cars and the waltz or tango we must dance between them. We are torn, however, between looking at an old man who beckons to us from the kerb or from the terrace of the café opposite as we conscientiously look left and right, turning the man into a blur as we struggle to get our bearings. Worse still, as we look left, look right, we are faced with the impossibility of choosing wisely: to the right, the boulevard is bathed in sunlight, enticing yet heartrending, to the left, dusk has already swathed the trees in a mournful yet soothing veil. And so, even as we glance back towards the old man, allowing ourselves to be guided by him, we invariably arrive somewhere other than where we wished to be, perhaps somewhere other than where we should have landed.

The Wise Old Man

For Zdeněk Vašíček

WE ARE IN A BISTRO OR A RESTAURANT, we are on our own, but not alone; the wise old man is with us, we need only peer through the half-light to see him. He too is on his own, but it hardly troubles him, content as he is with his wise old face, his freshly laundered shirt. He knows everything, has seen everything; and yet he pays careful attention to the wine he sips, to the soup he stirs, to the chives he carefully chops and adds to it—as though everything depended on it; when he gets up to leave, he will pay careful attention to the crease in his hat. The simple concentration he brings to being alone is enough to impart on us a crumb of his wisdom; he is there with us and for us.

It is true that it takes little—perhaps just one more glass—for everything to change. As we look up again at the old man, we catch him winking foolishly, attempting to catch some other diner's eye, or waving to everyone in the room; he cannot stop himself from muttering and nodding in agreement with what he says. He looks as though he has known nothing, has seen nothing, that he knows only how to be a nuisance, the wise old man has given way to the stupid old fool.

The Beautiful Woman

Travelling on a tram, or walking down the street we glance to one side and suddenly get a shock. We turn away quickly, but it gapes beside us still like a leering wound; there she is, a woman whose every gesture speaks to us, tenders us a secret invitation, her russet hair tied back with a clasp, the sidelong sparkle of two green eyes, the inrush of breath beneath her skin, between her parted lips. We take our courage in both hands and study the woman more intently, hoping against hope to find her wanting; but it is worse than we imagined, everything seems to confirm our conviction that with this woman we might experience some vital encounter that so far has treacherously eluded us. Her intimate gesture to the man with her reaches us with the same precision as the faraway look she bestows on those around her; as we mentally undress her, sliding along her skin towards the hollow of her belly, we realise with terrifying certainty that there, in that darkness, we might discover something else, something without which we know nothing.

Then, suddenly, the light shifts, the tram (the street) turns a corner, pale shafts of sunlight pierce the clouds—and everything is different. The woman's lips, we now notice, are marked by a line of weakness, the skin beneath her blouse betrays a slightly sour dampness almost like that of an old maid; doubtless she is also a faultfinder, a prig, a prude, God alone knows what she really has between her thighs. And yet we are not relieved for the void left by the beauty we glimpsed a moment before is more intense than the idea that it is unattainable; having already steeled ourselves to suffer vainly, the sudden disappearance of that ravishing beauty brings a new torment into the world. The hollow into which our shrivelled Valda pastilles vainly tumble is not merely a mysterious snare, a vice formed by two hips, it is the gaping of the cosmos itself.

The Storm

A STORM IS APPROACHING, the wind whips up, imploring the grave old men who stand at their windows in mute homage to it; in the distance a *Titanic* has reappeared on the murky seas, tossed about by the waves. As the light fails, lightning flashes illuminate the most desolate clearings, bringing to life dark hulking wrecks in their suburban pens, lighting up the old submarine at anchor near a quay in London making its waxwork crew seem paler still. Inside, the lightning flashes cause even the secret step at the top of the staircase to glow; outside they reveal, like a sudden apparition, the fool standing on the corner. A storm is both a firework display and a war, sometimes it is the transition between one and the other; it frustrates our expectations, distracts us from everyday tasks to speak to us of weightier subjects, in particular the fact that we do not haunt this world alone, nor entirely unwatched. Even a lightning-rod above our heads does not make the storm any less urgent; it merely displaces its centre of gravity towards the spectacle outside our windows and underscores the storm as something of an unexpected revelation. It is true we only experience it fully if it encircles and threatens us—just as we more truly savour red meat when, in its bleeding mass, we are confronted by our own death.

With its oblique light which, all of a sudden, causes shadows and corners to shift, moving the furniture in an office, the notebook on the desk, the pile of pencils in the drawer, lightning can bring to the surface a city hidden deep within the city. The air magnetised by the storm crackling amid the bolts of fabric in a shop in the dead of night is the true secret, the true heart of things, of the city and of the world. In prelude to a summer storm, the clouds will sometimes spend the afternoon endlessly chasing each other, shot through by sunlight which spends long moments playing with the least crumb, the smallest scrap of paper in the house—as much, one might say, to impart to each object a separate meaning as to reveal the meaning common to them all, uniting them into a tremulous whole. When at last the storm breaks, at the close of day, lightning flashes thumb through the blackened shrubs in the garden bringing forth a flash of unfamiliar thighs like the hidden meaning of all books. As the storm abates, the room—geometer moths fluttering through its open windows to bump into the lampshade—is not the haven it appears to be; no more a protective home than the gaping sex of the night sky. While in the distance, where the storm finally falls silent in a few last flashes of lightning, a welcoming living room and an enticing boudoir are revealed lit up side by side, perhaps, the respiration of the room revealing only their absence, like the one true centre.

Going In

For Puiu and Marina

THE COURTYARD BEYOND an unfamiliar doorway, how it glistens in the rain or glimmers in the sunlight, is an invitation to go inside and a promise; beyond the dustbin which rears up behind the peeling paint of a low wall, beyond the stair rod, beyond the rustling tree, we imagine we may discover a whole new world, perhaps rediscover a chapter of its hidden past. Yielding to temptation, we step through the doorway and walk towards the courtyard, but hardly have we taken the first few steps when we begin to slow; the more the courtyard unfolds before us, the less its promise is fulfilled; the low wall stretches out from the dustbin towards a less than welcoming rubbish heap, a van is parked arrogantly beside the stair rod and the tree. The world we seek was there in the scene framed by the doorway, but there is no trace of it in the courtyard; we have entered only to be disappointed: it only remains for us to leave. Sometimes, once outside the building again, we discover what we did not find inside smiling innocently down on us from the bare bricks of the façade …

On a rainy night with a female friend we step into a bar on the outskirts of an unfamiliar city and stumble on a local rock star in full-throated howl, surrounded by a group of her fans. We listen for a few minutes then suddenly our young companion moves forward, steps up to the singer and launches into a beautiful howl of her own, transforming the first girl's solo into a duet. People crowd around our friend, even the singer is forced to admit that she is good; we can be proud, she has truly made an entrance in the bar.

A summer landscape—open in every sense—is an inaccessible room *par excellence* in that it invites us to step simultaneously from every point. Only a painter succeeds in part in doing so as he sets up his easel before it, and from a distance, little by little, explores the landscape with short careful brushstrokes.

Loneliness

THE PAINTER WHO RISES EARLY, takes his flask, puts on his straw hat and heads off to paint in the fresh air, turns his back on us. And yet, later, as he plants his easel on the edge of a field and confronts the landscape spread out before him, patiently comes to know it, surveys and tames its expanse, facing the desert of the glorious day alone, he does so on our behalf, and walks beside us with every stroke he manages to wrest from his brush. At night, an actor in the theatre is happy to address himself to us, to attempt to seduce us, to curry favour, yet we find his attention increasingly overpowering—we want him to hurry up and finish so we can go somewhere and sit down to an honest dinner.

A void of irreparable loneliness opens up in the midst of even the wildest parties, in the fatal interlude when we step outside with a lady while in the next room the party carries on. Only love—and the strait gate of the lady—makes it possible for us to enter the world, and yet just as surely cut us off from it. We do not venture far, the voices and the chatter follow us into the bedroom and after a moment we begin to long to go back to the party. But even this only serves to deepen the paradox it reveals; the party is as incomplete without the lady as lovemaking is without the knowledge that friends are having a good time. It is an impossibility as irrefutable as it is difficult to grasp, a little like the impossibility of imagining both the boundlessness and the boundaries of the cosmos.

Having dinner with a lover on a terrace somewhere, surrounded by the murmuring night-time traffic of a foreign city, we inhabit the world together, we are almost complete; for the moment to be perfect, we need only mention the friends we have left behind, talk about their tics, their gestures, and as we talk we bring them leastways to our table from afar. We call our friends to us, too, during our solitary night-time walks, we feel less alone simply at the thought that they too are wandering somewhere at the far end of the night. Everything we do, everything we experience belongs now to her, to our love; and yet our friends continue to slip between us, to drink from our glasses, to try to persuade us to move on to another bar. Happily, on our way back, a sudden storm gives us reason to grasp our lover's shoulder, numb with cold we need only embrace the fear in her shivering body for our lonelinesses at least to become one.

Friendship

For Honza, Prokop and Standa

It is possible to think of friendship as a less spectacular form of love, less painful, less deadly but equally heartening. But hardly have we flushed out the partners-in-crime, the alter egos of our friends that breathe life into our 'me', when they reveal themselves to be secret rivals—funnier than we are, more talented, more popular with girls and with our common masters. Daringly, they climb a rock to dive from the summit into the water, they goad us, preferring purple to our favourite colour green, they all but become enemies; the fact that they do not share our predilections, rather than a desirable trait, is an inexplicable betrayal.

We are happy to be disloyal to ourselves; we are present without truly being present, with our friends and without them, now fighting with them, now making up; we stand shoulder to shoulder with them in a duel that is lost before it has begun, but we do so from a safe distance; when we allow our friends to triumph at some party, they congratulate us on our brilliant performance. Our time flies and stagnates, headlong we rush forward, only to turn in circles around a single moment as around an empty bowl. At least in doing so we can raise a glass with our friends in tribute to the mists in which we all lose our way, the shaky drawing of existence in greys vaguely strange and familiar.

Almost

NEARLY, ALMOST: DISCRETE YET CRUCIAL words which can immediately sum up and say *everything*. The *little touch* of lemon rind we add will put the finishing touch to the mayonnaise, just as it will put the finishing touch to our mastery of cooking; the oyster is a rare delicacy precisely because it is nothing more than a little albumen, barely flavoured, almost nothing. We have almost triumphed, nearly come to the point, almost understood everything; it was a near thing that we ever existed.

Disappointment

WHEN A MUCH-LOVED mountaineering friend—a conductor always ready to break into a ballad on his return from an expedition—saw the rock he had been trying to grab slip away from him before he fell, he must have been profoundly *disappointed*.[9]

Stuck

You were sitting on the potty in the kitchen when suddenly, paralysed by the presence of a maid in the bathroom next door, you couldn't go; you were stuck. As I closed the gate to the courtyard, a vicious mutt appeared opposite, motionless, but growling menacingly: I too was stuck. All of us, even now, find ourselves stuck in mid-sentence, in the middle of a street, even time seizes up: the letter to which we have been waiting impatiently for a reply still lies unposted, on our desk; sometimes we see it through the open window, flipped over by a mocking gust of wind. Stuck in time as between two locked gates, we cannot go back, while up ahead, suddenly, there is nothing but fog; fruitlessly we struggle to find a reason to finish the sentence, the solo, to go on pushing, to cross the courtyard or the street. Better to remain stuck here counting the passing cars; we probably have nothing to say except our stammering, the poem begins and ends with the first line which can simply be repeated endlessly. We wanted to wave, to say hello, to draw attention to ourselves and show that we are here; we have done so.

We do not even know how old we are, we have learnt nothing, and everything is behind us now; the things around us, cars, friends, strangers passing by, all sink back slowly into themselves, growing darker now like a film stuck in a projector. Nothing leads anywhere, the grey of afternoon stretches away with the four winds; life is but a plateau where we glance about wildly.

Sometimes, even the landscape suddenly disappears like a spring that has run dry, the overgrown strip on the edge of a field and the ribbon of the path evaporate into mist and silence: it is finished, no more landscape. All that remains is to lie in wait on some distant doorstep and watch it alternate, now there, now absent, revocable as existence.

An Unfamiliar Bathroom

B<small>EFORE GOING INTO AN UNKNOWN BATHROOM</small>, we borrow a towel and a washcloth from our hosts; but we are careful not to ask what awaits us behind the door, attempting to discover for ourselves the hidden order of the place, the location of the dryers, the light switches, the workings of the shower. Our exploration however lasts longer than expected, we search in vain for the waste basket and the nail file, we cannot quite understand the unfamiliar way in which things are organised. We are almost on the point of calling out to our hosts and asking how the hell things are organised and why, and where they got the idea to organise things this way rather than another. Would they also know why and how to go on living?

Undressing

As we undress before making love, already turned towards the other, we review what little we have to offer, incredulous and surprised that our partner can take this for uncharted territory—that we are permitted to make it one with her charms. Undressing, again, when we are alone, faintly moved, we see only our own fragility, we sympathise with it and are prepared to believe, after all, that it will win out over the self-confidence of the more muscled people around us.

The Enemy

THE ENEMY IS NOT THE PERSON who bars our path nor the policeman who come to haul us away; no—the enemy slips into our home early in the morning like an old acquaintance, calls us by our first name, sits on the edge of our bed, slaps us companionably on the belly. He knows better than we how he should behave in the world, force-feeds us advice, and tells jokes as though we enjoyed them.

Sometimes, we envy him the promptness with which he rushes to the doll in its nappy—having barely smelled the ammonia in its hair—we are jealous of his boldness at diving into a trench and keeping his head down, the speed with which he forgets and moves on to something else. But even he is merely a stand in; our true enemy, his master, keeps us waiting, gauging the weight of his cudgel, postponing the fatal blow he is preparing to deal us. Can it be that he is afraid of the miniscule but indelible red dot which our pin will leave upon his forehead during the attack?

The Main Entrance

WE ARE BOTH JEALOUS AND SUPPORTIVE of those whose time comes before ours, who collect their belongings and are free to leave the hospital or the barracks; they leave in our place, as to some test we hope they will not fail. We hold our breath: hoping they will make it through the front door without a hitch, step into the street and calmly look about them, board their bus, their train, and stepping off, cross the threshold of their house, of their apartment. There, we hope they will find what, holed up here, we talked about as a lost paradise, treat it with the respect it deserves, cherish the everyday so that it does not lose its lustre: the shopping trips, the walks, the bedroom whispers, the catcalls with friends, the cigarette smoked in silence in the kitchen. But a few days later, we find them back at the main entrance, looking regretfully behind them, they send for us to chat awhile, ask us what has been going on here, *at our place*; it is almost as though they miss the place, or as if they have discovered that they were not much missed in the home they went back to. One thing is certain: they have allowed what was waiting for them there to close around them, like the walls of a hospital or of a barracks, they have failed the test. They may pretend that they have passed, but in their defence they offer only uninspired circumstantial evidence which even they do not believe—a photograph, a snapshot of a wedding cake eaten long ago, sometimes simply their identity card; but in their eyes we see their one burning desire: never to have to leave again, to stay here forever by the main entrance. Even the convicts released from the Guyana penal colony, we are told, used to build their house facing the gaol as though this view is enough to last them the rest of their days; tourists sitting on the terrace of Les Deux Magots meekly resign themselves to gazing at the terrace opposite where the ugly faces of other tourists block their view like faithful echoes of their own.

Those who left before us have doubly failed, because they failed to pass the test and because they themselves rushed back to let us know. For our part, we are all the more determined, we vow that *we will never come back to this door,*—even for them—not even if we should die in a ditch. But will we know how to recognise our own door in time?

The Homecoming

To Jan Gabriel (and to Prokop)

PERHAPS EVEN WAR, we speculate with a friend, will be redeemed by coming home from war, by the glory and the relief of that instant when we are the cigarette we smoke, standing on a tank, riding into a city, filled with hope, gazing around us at the streets and the young girls applauding us from the pavements. Doubtless even the meaning of a journey or a prolonged interlude out in the world is only truly known when we return home, when we are reunited with everyday objects—their familiarity springing back like trampled grass—and through the conversations in which we tell of our experiences and discover what has been happening here in our absence: how the neighbours' daughter has blossomed or grown fat, how the simpleton across the road has grown up to be a conman.

Even a Sunday family outing only began to truly come alive after we had survived it and when, back home, we heard the dull roar of the cycle track out beyond the garden where the last race was finishing. Even our night-time peregrinations are crowned only by morning and the astonishment with which, when we return home and turn our attention to the objects we find hidden deep inside the sofa, envying them the peaceful night they spent here in our stead.

At the end of a long summer's route, after exhausting journeys on night trains and vain attempts to catch a glimpse of the woman—and perhaps the shadow of some absent enemy—we set out to meet in the meadows, as we come back to the city at the close of another sweltering Sunday, we imagine our journey to have been a fatal error since what we looked for in vain elsewhere seems to radiate here whole and entire, in the façades of the buildings filled with warmth, in the deserted streets where the sound of a teaspoon falling in the distance rings out like a call. Those who spend their Sundays in the city sometimes have only to head out to a *brasserie* to buy beer, with no other company than their flapping slippers, to find themselves on a journey around the world.

Around the World

For Jacques Lacarrière

A BEAUTIFUL DAY SPREADS OUT once more before us and once more we wonder what to do with it and *where* we should go to find it. We have but one choice—to go around the world, to the ends of the earth. We should leave right now, without even taking the time to change out of our slippers, armed with the jug with which we set out to buy beer. Now, we need simply trust to the lies and lures we will encounter along the way—sometimes before we ever reach the *brasserie*—and our little stroll through the streets will carry on for years and lead us to the far antipodes. Within a few days, we will come upon our first fireball in the meadows, and somewhere along the way we will stumble on the end of the world and emerge unscathed; in the time it takes to think about it, we will have turned the corner, still in working condition.

We stop only once, by the roadside near a football pitch where the sunlit grass stretching out towards the horizon seems to point the way; now we need only let ourselves be guided, cross the pitch following the trajectory of the goal that went astray. We still have some distance to cover, we are passed from one sunny day to the next like a baton, before coming back onto the same pitch and recognising the other goal in the one from which we started.

The South

Everyone knows how things are set in motion: suddenly, the weather is beautiful, we breathe the soft air and the aroma of freshly ground coffee, we notice that the most important thing, that which we most need, is missing. Everything urges us on to go and join it; the city itself, open now as far as the subdued brightness of the paddocks on the *périphérique*, rings out with the call of the distant South where *something* is waiting for us, something which begins perhaps in a nearby suburb, behind a quiet church a few scant feet away. To know happiness, we need only go there, need only follow the secret current of cool air in the sweltering sky, skirt the footpaths where small tables have already been set for lunch, find a quiet tavern and, at the end of the hallway, a staircase that rises to a terrace where a cheerful young girl is spraying white, freshly laundered sheets before ironing them; but first, as an obligatory detour, we cut through a narrow alleyway, through a shadowy shop there to silently greet the men's hats dozing on the shelves. Buoyed up by our mute presence, the southern girl takes the laundry from her basket, we can smell the caress of perfumed soap and silken skin and as we do so, we see the lowering storm and the approaching dusk. All that remains is to know whether the storm will provide the vital element to make our happiness complete, making it possible for us to help the girl to snatch the laundry from the washing line and rehang it in the half-light of a loft—or whether, at the first clap of thunder, the South will once more disappear forever.

Walls and Fences

For Honza

THE OLD WALL HIDES NOTHING FROM US, it is not even an obstacle; it is merely a journey's end waiting to be discovered behind the film of drizzle which, from a distance, we watched fall against the wall as in front of a screen. In fact, the moment we stop before the wall, we begin a new journey, a patient, painstaking exploration of its uneven bulk, the rich shades and details of the cracks, the crevices, the patches of damp through which we plunge into the wall to the further recesses of its memory. On its own, a ramshackle wooden fence forms an intriguing screen, which urges us to look behind and discover its mysteries or promises, what fantastical sperm whale or zeppelin swells behind it in secret, preparing to lift its dark head above the fence; what logs lie piled up there, what timbers lie in heaps with which to build new fences? The more we examine it, the more the fence makes us suspect what things lie behind it, perhaps we shall even see a whole strange city flower there. It can be seen in the tattered scraps of old posters stuck to the planks, it is mapped out already in the knots, in the grain of the wood.

Details

For Petr Hruška

Hardly had we glanced around that we immediately began to carefully study everything, all the fantastical details among which we find ourselves—if only to understand why. Every board in the fence and every nail, every knot in the grain and every speck of dust in every knot, the whole fence, plank after plank, to the last thistle growing at the base, to the last splinter, chalk mark, mud spatter. Was all this not simply a secret preparation for the duty we had to perform in the detailed examination of the female body, the surprising curves and angles, fragrant nooks and folds, warm borders, clefts, the pink groundswell surging from beneath tufts of wiry or of downy hair?

It must be so, unless perhaps the opposite is true: that our detailed discoveries of the female form made it possible for us to broach the physical world and there take root among the thistles and the nettles, the planks and cobwebs? Whatever the case, it is impossible for us to separate the two; even our dearest friends, in spite of what they might think, are barely distinguishable from the details of the bracelets and the clothes they wear. We love them, bonnets and earrings and all, we nuzzle them beneath their finery just as we nuzzle the soft silk; lovemaking does not begin with removing one's clothes, it is a constant, endless gliding from detail to detail, from the cold fur coat to the warm ear, from the rustle of a stocking to the warmth of a thigh, details which love connects one to another so as to knit the world together for a moment.

Lovemaking

THE POET STOPS THE CAR, leaps out, runs to the nearest tree by the roadside, shakes it, pounds it with his fists and howls that he wants a woman, that he *needs* her right here right now. Undoubtedly he feels a need, but perhaps he is also trying, demonstrating his masculinity, proving how obsessed he is. Though it is something that everyone does—or at least tries to do—we do not do it with the same talent or the same conviction. It is true that lovemaking concerns everyone and through it reveals their relationship with the world—even those who think of it as a pitiful form of gymnastics, or those who dream about it more than they do it; there is no avoiding it, we are all in some way bound to it, but it is precisely this which obscures the significance it assumes for us.

Some treat lovemaking as a sport, others as a form of revenge, for some it is a duty, for others a distraction, a form of self-punishment, a mystical ecstasy, a terrorist act, a means of taking control or of overcoming loneliness, one thinks of it merely as a tribute to the moment and to the night city, another, perhaps, thinks of it as an expression of love. And yet we all seem to share one passion, a desire to slip, through lovemaking, into a different space: into a different body, a different life, beyond the bounds of contemporary mores, into the deepest depths of the night. In fact, we share our bed with three distinct individuals—an actual woman, the ideal woman we seek in her, and the night personified; if in the individual we sometimes discover only her loneliness, the second merges so completely with the ambient night that we come through it with her by our side. Lovemaking also gives us a glimpse of unknown facets of our physical being; the idle chatter after lovemaking as we both slide towards sleep deepens our intimacy with the woman whom, among all living creatures, we are closest to.

And yet the full meaning of things is revealed only by the need to abandon elsewhere for here; to leave the distant spaces glimpsed—and our transient desire to embrace their strangeness—to return to those whom we know, to the boundaries and the commonplace of our two bodies and our shared life. This coming to earth spares no one, not even the distant princess, who, when we both took wing, seemed closer to us, proving herself to be less aloof, almost as fragile and as mad as we are; for all of her charms, her perfumes, her sparkling eyes, her languid gestures, as she gathers up her clothes before taking coffee with us, she is as circumscribed by her own limits as everyone else. To make love is to cross a frontier, to rebel against the established order, but it is not an escape; it distracts us from our resolutions only so that we may admit them to ourselves, the journey through space it opens up before us expands our humdrum existence and becomes a celebration given in its honour.

(The entirety of our journey in the company of others is already contained—and condensed—into the first glance we exchange with them, a glance which reveals not only future friends but the availability and desire of possible partners, just as it allows us to predict that others will be enemies or strangers. From the outset, every nascent relationship reveals its individual *luminosity*, its tragic or conciliatory nature; otherwise it is simply a proposition to be developed, like a twist of paper whose singular flower will bloom only when it is dipped into the tide of time. Destiny has been revealed to us, but the details are vague—the jaggedness of the rock in the background, the passion with which we will kiss in front of it, the wildness of the rain that will put an end to—or prolong—our kisses, all these are hidden still beyond the horizon. And yet, in that first glance is a glimmer of truth which reveals only a possible, predetermined world, that same truth which little by little, in spite of the dreams of utopians, reveals the inexorable march of History.)

Weight

For Marek Stašek

A COUNTRY BISTRO in the first years of the last century. Looking at it, we can feel the tingle of *pastis* in glasses, rubbed like concealer against the skin of time, the weight of jackets on bodies and the weightlessness of the passing of time.

The Concert

For Tomáš Paul

WE ARE LISTENING TO A CONCERT—or trying to listen—but are constantly distracted from its harmonious swell by the static image of the coats the musicians have abandoned in their dressing room. Moreover, it is the performers who distract us, as they turn the pages of their scores, screw up their faces, flush, mop the sweat from their brows; we do not know what to do, should we follow the music they are playing or the curious spectacle they are spiritedly performing while they play? Only with time will we understand what the concert brings to the music precisely because of the details its setting—and the transience of the event—which circumscribes it and restrict it despite the music's ambition to transport us elsewhere, to a place beyond space and time. In this, the tentative sounds of the instruments tuning up, the prelude to the orchestra's attack, are as much part of the performance as the applause which swells to fill the hall as the concert ends: it is only by allowing the music to rise above the rippling murmurs and rustling and to fade away again that these two incidental accidents cause its metaphysical nature to appear. It is true that the only worthwhile concert we ever heard was on an old record which someone in a villa near our campsite unwittingly played to help us get to sleep, whose crackle and hiss, as it drifted towards us, mingled with the night-time murmurs of the forest.

The Solo

For Honza

SOMEONE WHO TAKES A SOLO plays for the others, struts, rails against the world, against himself, and gloriously sacrifices himself in their place. In return, he may then rejoin the throng from which he so courageously sprang, set his patent-leather shoe next to his neighbour's trainer and unwrap his croissant next to his neighbour's sandwich. The morning after a hard night's drinking, during the cut-throat joke-telling around the breakfast table by which each of us in turn attempts to ward off the mounting anxiety, a perfect solo may be a single well-chosen word. And it is to take a solo, too, that we set out for a walk, though it may take our whole life.

The Revolving Door

Passing through the vast hallway of a bank or a hotel, we may be there with other visitors—perhaps even with close friends—but we move away from them, and from ourselves. Hardly have our eyes met when, suddenly weightless, they float away in all directions beneath the high ceiling, in the half-light into which comes only the faint echo of the outside world; the perpetual ebb and flow of the seas, of the soles scraping the pavements, retreating again in a faint backwash, almost a sigh. A single eyelid blinks in welcome to us from the far end of the lobby: the revolving door where those who come in or go out, simple silhouettes, constantly vanish into the tremulous daylight. In this flickering light even the hallway loses its individual traits, it resounds with the echoes of other halls in banks or post offices, other courtyards, other waiting rooms, in railway stations and ports, and with the never-ending comings and goings of the crowds trudging through; reunited with these distant spaces, the lobby steps outside of time with them, pools its memory with theirs in a single immemorial wave. Woven from shadows and light, it is now simply a place of expectancy, of transfusion—of night into day and back again—an ethereal hall above which the intrigues of every drama emerges and is resolved in the same moment.

As we are leaving—already feeling the breath of an impatient crowd at our back—the revolving door hollows out an empty space before us. It allows us to do a little dance with the space, transforming our departure into a moment of weightlessness during which we lose our bearings, so much so that in the world outside everywhere we look offers astonishment. We do not even know where the door will eject us, forward or backward, north or south, whether we will rise to the surface or dive to the depths; we reappear on stage like a laugh or a sneeze erupting suddenly from the wings.

The Right Knife and the Missing Weight

To Dominique and Georges-Henri Martin

A REAL HOME IS NOT NECESSARILY MARKED by the shine of its accessories, the panoply of tools carefully arranged in a gleaming, spotless cellar or a kitchen whose very neatness often makes it seem frozen, lifeless as a mausoleum. On the contrary, one of the surest signs of a real home—of the life—is a 'good knife', hidden in a drawer somewhere which, each time it is needed, has to be found: a tense ritual involving everyone present that is an integral part of the roast chicken or beef the knife is needed to carve. It is not enough to find the knife, to extricate it from the jingling confusion of blunt, nameless and misleading knives; everyone must agree that this is the right knife, reconcile the conflicting opinions that quickly arise, remember that the thin knife has proved itself to have a better blade than the heavier knife though the handles are the same size and made of the same dark wood …

The person who has been appointed to carve—often following another tense ritual—now brandishes not merely a knife, but a sceptre emblematic of shared family memory, temporarily reprieved from the oblivion by this search.

Another symbol of this shared memory—and another sign of a real home—can be something missing: the small hollow in the wooden stand of the old-fashion weighing scales which holds the line of small brass weights of ever decreasing size. In any self-respecting home, the last—and only this one—will be an empty space, the weight it should contain now simply a theoretical presence, a ghost. And yet it is this weight which most intrigues us, which we most long to touch, to examine; we can almost feel the almost insubstantial mass in our hands when all the while the tiny empty hollow gazes at us with unfathomable sadness. It prompts us to endless speculations about what might have happened to it, about the long forgotten moment, buried in the depths of family history, when it was lost, and in doing so the missing weight reaffirms its presence, reawakens memory. By the immateriality with which its microscopic mass is reabsorbed at the far end of the scale, it seems to bear witness to some secret link between the visible and the invisible and to hint that the one is a seamless continuation of the other.

The Fish Soup[10]

For Matěj

WE SPEND A LONG TIME PREPARING IT, almost the whole afternoon on Christmas Day. As we do so, we carefully examine the ingenious anatomy of the heads of the hen carp we crumble into the liquid, just as, when the soup is ready, the subtle balanced flavours—in noble concentration—reveal the riches of the muddy world the carp knew when they were alive. Everyone waits impatiently for the soup to be ready, we love it so much that perhaps it is the only reason we celebrate Christmas; next to this, even the presents are simply guests waiting in the doorway, looking shyly towards the centre of the room where the Fish Soup takes pride of place, like a pretty cousin in a grey dress. Together we sing its praises, but each of us savours it alone, lingering over it as over our own destiny. The following day, having had time to rest a while, it is even more delicious, although already there is nothing left but a greyish ring around the pot, which we wash away with a sigh, the pretty cousin in her horse-drawn carriage is now only a pinprick on the horizon, inexorably drawn to her homeland in the Russian steppes. We remind ourselves that at least, with luck, we will see her again next year, and suddenly we are waiting impatiently.

Nothing is more miraculous than Czech Fish Soup, and nothing more completely proves that such a miracle is as possible as it is impossible to preserve.

Meaning

Savoured with my *pigeon aux baies sauvages*, the Barolo from the cellars of Banfi reveals its full meaning.

The Terrace

T HE GENTLE SHIVER OF A TABLECLOTH on a restaurant terrace momentarily wards off the wave of emptiness that assails us, the snapping of the awning suddenly makes the sky itself boom, right here, above our heads.

The Airship

For George and Mila

TIME WAS, WHEN LONG AGO a hot-air balloon rose above Rodez, above the dizzying peak on whose summit the town stands, a farmer from the nearby valleys who chanced to glance up at the heavens would have got the shock of his life. Even today, the sight of an airship fills us with wonder. When a grey airship emerges from a bank of cloud over Lisbon, like a suddenly sovereign scrap of mist, the whole grey city glides with it somewhere within us, paying us a visit. A passing airship makes the skies of Paris or New York catch its breath. As, in the distance, the oblong shape passes behind a bridge near to the Eiffel Tower, it propels the city out of time and—to our relief—draws it towards the horizon as if to tow it back into the depths of memory, to the distant dawn of the century. The blimp above Central Park momentarily appeases both the clamour of the city and our regret at knowing so little of the spaces over which the airship traces its peaceful arc.

Even the advertisement that the blimp serves to display does not bother us, seeming as it does to be a part of the more vital and more cosmic message which the airship communicates by its very motion. The legend *Goodyear* is no longer simply a brand of tyres, an instruction to drive meekly on the motorways, among the flock; it invites us to take the whole year as a holiday, to join the chosen few the airship carries above our heads. We can imagine every detail, the glittering people, well turned out, the gentlemen's ostentatious caps, the ladies' bonnets lifted by the breeze, the taut elastic of their chin straps, the billowing dresses, the cheerful bobbing of bottles in baskets filled with delicacies—to say nothing of the flushed faces, the impassioned glances, the plunging *décolletés*: a year spent exploring Paradise in an uninterrupted succession of close-ups. The trip no doubt also includes a number of dramatic incidents, sometimes the aeronauts descend towards a mountain top there to deposit a cold body and with it the keys to a car.

The Terminus

For Giovanni Catelli

As we arrive, the day grows mute beneath the noonday hush or the impending twilight, the tram now simply loops around a length of track, wiping the sky from its quivering perch hugging the horizon where suburban kitchen gardens appear suddenly like calm oases. Further off, the static backcloth heralds a storm this afternoon or clear skies tomorrow, a new paling, a new crack in History; the tram has described a semi-circle and comes into the station facing the other way, drawing alongside a large box filled with sand as though to pass the baton. The driver climbs down from his cabin, flips the sign on the windshield, once more nothing has happened, everything can be wiped away and transformed into its opposite, a faint gleam glides simultaneously to the front and back of the carriage roof, the cabbages cooking in the flowerbeds share out the infinite destinies of the world with the sandbox, heavy now with rain. There is a pause, a respite; the tram-driver, transformed from busy skipper to serene smoker, draws on his cigarette, hero of the moment, with only the prestige of the signal box to lean against, and the uniform of grey fabric which he offers to the day in our stead.

And yet nothing terminates at the terminus; the rails have led the city here—to this perimeter which they circumscribe, obliterated now by twilight, and beyond which they stream into the suburbs—the better to see itself from afar, to gauge its true measure, before it returns, with the tram, all the more committed to itself and to the clamour of stories which simmer together in its melting pot.

On the Move

It is forbidden to speak to the driver while the bus is moving, but the embargo itself proves how tempting it is: to talk to the driver during the journey, to the goalie about how the match is going, to call to the actors from the wings during the play. Drive them, play with them a little, but also make them a part of our game, our journey so that they can see themselves; all of this, here and now, on the move. If, in the middle of the concert, it is difficult to go and talk to the band leader in person, at least chat to the drummer. In a world without god, it is only natural when at table to want to share some human conversation with the waiter and the chef before the restaurant closes and they in turn treacherously cast us out into the night.

The View

ONLY ON THE EDGE OF THE FOREST does nature offer us a real view, with the slope at our feet, bathed in sunlight like an amphitheatre, and the half-light of the wings at our back. Sometimes we find a small wooden lookout tower propped against a tree like a ladder waiting to board passengers onto a hot-air balloon or some future Ark. We climb to the top, for the sake of it, but climb down again immediately; the view from the top broadened our horizon but took us too far from the others and from the view we came to contemplate on the edge of the forest. The view is inseparable from the landscape itself, it would be incomplete if it did not remind us that we are a part of what we look at. It also encompasses the view from the watchtower towards which we turn now, studying it as though it were destined only to be seen from below, waiting for an absent watcher to return.

Absence

1

They say that when Eiffel climbed his tower for the first time to view Paris from above, he marvelled at the panorama but for one thing; he could not see the Eiffel Tower. When we first fall in love with a woman, her charm, her breath, the fire in her eyes and the scent of her skin mingle for us with everything such that all things are obliterated; the whole world is but a hazy counterpart to our love. When we fall out of love, on the other hand, the world re-emerges but as though absent from itself, shorn of the Eiffel Tower which alone made it recognisable.

2

When, as for some pressing reason beyond her control, our companion goes home before us, leaving the town (the village) where together, we retreated from the world for a few days, the landscape enfolds us with an attentive but almost intimidated clarity; blood drains away, all that remains, suddenly arid, is the bed of a universal vastness, the nakedness of railway tracks stretching towards the horizon, along the deserted platforms. Although we shared with our companion only a thin thread of excitement in the darkness, a last fracture before the silence, everything then was speech where now we are confronted by the muteness of objects, the newness they rediscover with the sole intention of taking it nowhere but blindly remaining here within her. Each object, in the image of that which is no longer here, requires meticulous treatment—from the toothpick snatched from a bar to the parapet of a bridge we lean on for support—but each offers to the touch only a small quantity of mute matter. Though new and accessible again, as though untouched, the real shuns our caress like a statue in the winter air cast from absent snow.

When, on the other hand, we unexpectedly go back to the scene of revelry and merrymaking which, an hour earlier, we thought we had left for good—already excited at the idea of rediscovering the warmth we found it so difficult to leave behind—we discover only an astounding ignorance of our absence: the party is in full swing, all the more merry for the fact that it is sufficient unto itself, like the world which in advance has decided to shamelessly go about its tiring business without us.

The Bump

Bumping into others can result in a dull thud, or can jolt us like a flash of inspiration, sometimes for years to come. The impossibility of making ourselves understood is so crushing that it all but relieves us of our duties to the world, leaving us to our own folly; being dazzled by another may cause us to break apart inside for a time, but they exhort us all the more insistently to put ourselves back together. A friend can give us a clap on the back so heartening it all but kills us; the low blow dealt by an enemy sometimes brings us back to the surface in a flash.

The Toothpick

For Michal Novotný

THE LOUT WHO STICKS IT between his teeth and sucks on it as he talks to us, trains the toothpick on us like a weapon. He who, having finished dinner, uses it discreetly screened by the palm of his hand, connects us with a wider space, the dining room opens out to include the expanse of the night-time railway station which he discovers, to his surprise, in his own mouth. On his deathbed, using a toothpick for the last time, the author of *Ubu Roi*, behind the palm of his hand, has already secretly turned it towards the future, and towards us, his orphans yet to come.

Good Taste

For František Listopad

As GEORGE SANDERS TAKES INGRID BERGMAN on a tour of his late uncle's house, he acknowledges that his relation had good taste; though he mumbles it between his teeth with the smile of a jaded man of the world, the admission seems no more important to him than his daily shower or his hankering for fine food. Is taste anything more than a personal *hobby horse*?

One thing is certain, the collars of certain jackets, with their grey, finely-woven fabric (made in England) are more suited to rain than others, when, standing beneath a canopy or an awning, collars are turned up and tower over the shoulders. The people with whom we most successfully share our sojourn in this world are those who, turning away from us, contemplate the puddles in the street with the most discreet glance.

Lunch

If a wedding reception is a feast, it is as much because of the number and rarity of the courses as for the fact that it continues into the evening. Even a simple lunch in the country can become a feast if we linger at the table, slip our jackets off, unbutton our shirts, uncork another bottle and help ourselves to seconds from the serving dishes, while the children, mouths crammed with biscuits, head off to play at the other end of the garden. We enjoy the afternoon simply by allowing it to slip lazily away, stretching lunchtime out until dinner, the midday meal sometimes slipping seamlessly into supper which we attack with renewed appetite—even those who were about to leave hesitate for a moment out of politeness—while the lady of the house, her hair redone, unearths hidden reserves in the fridge. Those here are strangers for the most part, we would never have met them had it not been for this lunch, but we are charmed by them; we listen gravely to what they say, laugh at their jokes and try to make them laugh in turn, together we try to set the world to rights. Suddenly we see them as accomplices, soul mates who share our taste in wines, in books, in cities, not realising that they are commonplace choices generally in favour and that we have mentioned we are passionate about them. The occasion is crowned by a smouldering look exchanged with one of the ladies present who comes over and whispers to us out of earshot of the others, as though arranging a tryst. The woman who accompanied us has the same experience; as we leave, taking with us the secret recipes, the travel tips confided by others, we feel as though we have been party to some indecent, immoral game which has opened up a new world to us. For only that can truly explain the seriousness with which we take down their addresses, and the fact that we will never see them again.

Pleasure

The idea comes to us like a sudden revelation; there is no need to think twice, it is decided: we are going to live life to the full. We turn on the heating in the middle of a cold summer without worrying, we take out a bottle and something to nibble despite the fact that it is late; in the bistro, the morning after a long drinking session, we treat ourselves to steak for breakfast. And immediately we are filled with a sense of triumph; the joy of having dared to break the chains of routine, of cause and effect, spreads through us so resolutely that it opens up the world before us. Unfortunately, it does not last, for after the first juicy mouthful, the steak simply serves to fill us up; the pleasure with which we opened the bottle dissipates; we barely manage to come out with a few anxious jokes that sound forced. There is nothing to be done: our joy was so intense that it instantly burnt itself out.

On another occasion, as we drink our wine, share a bed with a beautiful woman, or simply slip alone between cool sheets, telling ourselves that we are truly happy; hardly have we said the words than the sensation fades as though true happiness can only be glimpsed for a moment. Perhaps it exists only in memory as when, home from a party we turn to each other and say "that was fun, wasn't it". As though seeking to reassure. Sometimes, reading a diary or an old letter years after it was written, we realise that we must have been happy *then*—if only in comparison with our current misery. Even when we are truly caught up in the moment and it lasts, when we sink into love, into sleep or step out of the cold into a warm room and feel warmth creep over us, from without and within, our sense of wellbeing is whole but not complete. Even as we feel it suffuse us, still we feel another layer of happiness beneath which we cannot reach; a different—and more genuine—warmth which eludes us even as we diligently immerse ourselves, sinking our whole body into the warmth that fills the room—the only warmth available. Here is a warmth beyond our reach, trapped somewhere in some unknown elsewhere like the music hidden beneath music which from time to time we hear break the surface in the muted hums and cries with which an excited soloist—pianist or bassist[11]—accompanies himself.

We can hardly complain, we are *happy*, it is simply that we know that we could be happier. The gentlest Chinese girl hides a sister, who is gentler and dreamier still; the deepest sleep conceals a repose more complete, more refreshing—just as, even as we enjoy the pleasure of reading, we are tempted by the pleasure of setting down a book and breathing freely. Who knows, perhaps we ourselves, beyond the warm room, the life we share with those close to us, are seeking a different life, one which is ours and which we share, for a change, with people we barely know: the old men from the *taverna* somewhere in Italy, the guest at the wedding reception years ago, the friend whom we always picture in his bachelor apartment, in a foreign city, surrounded by piles of books and cassettes—but whom we speak to only occasionally, in vague terms, in a hotel lobby; the pasty Dubliner glimpsed in a dark corridor one rainy day, the beautiful redhead we met briefly one night in the *métro* and starred in a film with us that same night before we fell asleep.

Sometimes, we think these hidden depths are just the other side of the wall, in our neighbours' apartment when we hear them bustle about, imagining them wriggling around in perfect warmth compared to which our apartment is an icy waiting room; unless of course our neighbours are thinking the same thing about us, imagining that perfect warmth to be on our side of the wall. In any event, we reassure ourselves, no matter how much they turn up the heat, it won't last long, in a moment their jacket will slide off the piano again and the lid will grow cold from the blast of air which blows their window open.

(Some, you might say, offer a key to our inability to ever truly enjoy ourselves in the manner in which they fulfil their roles as parents, as they sternly advise their daughter to put an end to a flawed relationship; I'm sure you *do* love this boy, they admit, and maybe he is polite and honest; but you should never forget that there is *something more* to life. And perhaps they are right, we are even prepared to agree with them; there is certainly something more, something which we are waiting for and which waits for us. But what is that something and where will we find it? Even our parents will not tell us, merely following these remarks with a pointed silence. It is their daughter's duty to try and find out more, just as it is ours; we must go on searching, go on feeling our way. Were the parents thinking simply of hindsight, which lurks behind even the most perfect loves? What is still perfect, even in the eyes of an older and wiser aunt, when, in the half-light, she looks up towards the piano? Is the *something more* the alcove in which the aunt shares our bed in a dream beneath the roofs of some foreign city? Or is it the inaccessible kitchen of a restaurant and the chef who exquisitely and mysteriously takes care of us, before stepping out of the kitchen to reveal an unremarkable little man?)

The Law

IT IS AN IMPLACABLE LAW: the moment we open a book in order to read a favourite passage to a friend, it disappears without trace. Though we leaf through the book page by page, we only succeed in ruining the evening, for our friend and for ourselves: the passage has *disappeared* from the book. The only thing to do is set the book down and wait calmly, patiently for the passage to reappear—in practice this means we need only wait until our friend has left to reach for the book and it will slide to the floor and fall open at the page we were looking for. (Just as mistakes vanish from proofs when we try to correct them only to laugh in our faces when the finished book arrives.) It yet remains to discover the secret significance of this law and decide how much we are to blame: do we really want to read the passage aloud, have we not simply abandoned the idea at the last minute for fear that our friend would not appreciate it?

Heading out to a party in a dinner jacket, we vow not to let it get dirty. In doing so we invoke another implacable law which will transform good intentions into bad: not only will the dinner jacket get dirty, we will find ourselves using it to mop up a puddle in the toilet as though overcome by a fit of madness. And we will only appear to be upset: from the instant we vowed not to let the jacket get dirty, we have thought about nothing else.

The restaurant mysteriously glimmering on the edge of an old neighbourhood that we noticed as soon as we arrived, the gracefully run-down haberdashers almost opposite our hotel—these, to us, are the vital secrets of a foreign city; the excitement we feel about exploring the city becomes fixated on exploring these places. Every day we set out to visit them, but unforeseen last minute circumstances force us to reschedule. The day before our departure, we finally make it only to find the restaurant and the shop are closed. We feel relieved, of course—now we have a reason to come back.

Mothers and Daughters

For Sylvie Pagé

ONLY VISITING MOTHERS truly makes it possible to get to know a foreign city; for it to accept us, we must linger in the market watching burly women gutting fish, laughing at the jokes they fire at us like an oracle-fireball, we must present ourselves before the old landlady and allow her to decide if we are worthy to stay in her *auberge*. After the mother come the daughters, especially in the neighbouring cities of the North, Berlin, Frankfurt, Krakow. They move about in gaggles, so much so that alone they barely exist, at least to our eyes. It is impossible to tear one from the throng, to take her aside, it is always as a group that they arrive in a dim cellar bar or at a party, that they begin to dance around us, to babble at us like a flock of cheerful crows (though they are pale, they all wear black). It is as a group that they approach, rub against us, laughing and tickling each other and us; it is in groups that they dance, redo their hair, flatter the piano player, remove our ties and drag us onto the dance floor before vanishing once more into the night. Perhaps each one of them has her own life somewhere, a polished bathtub in a villa, a charming flat on a housing estate, a piggybank and a simple stock of snowy underwear. Perhaps they even hide beneath their skirts a beauty spot and a little tantalising Polish dirt in some unwashed intimate fold; but, beneath the clucking and the subdued brilliance of their *décolletés* which, as they tango, they offer as one to the night, it is almost impossible to tell. And it is they, if we humbly agree to play their game, who smooth our entrance into the city, offering us their precious blessing—if only by abstractedly adjusting the collar of our shirt as we dance.

New Temptations and Old Trousers

For Tomáš Frýbert

NO MATTER HOW MANY WE HAVE, there is always some—vitally important—book or record we are missing; even in those cities we know intimately, there is still one last—crucially important—place we have yet to visit. But this last quarry stubbornly eludes us—the book is out of print, the record is the only one of the series no longer available, we do not get to see the place we have never visited, either it is being renovated or we cannot find it. Happily, nothing makes life easier than a prey that proves inaccessible—for when we finally, by some miracle, manage to lay hands on it, our joy turns to fear: what new prey will be our target now?

In the wardrobe, on the other hand, we constantly come across old pairs of trousers or socks which mysteriously reappear though we are certain that we threw them away a long time ago. Suddenly unsure, we give them one last chance, perhaps they are still wearable, but when we try them on we simply discover we have been fooled again, forced to endure the same humiliation: the elastic of the socks is flaccid, the zip of the trousers permanently jammed.

Angrily, we take them off, but, curiously, put them back in the wardrobe vaguely telling ourselves that we will throw them out next time, as though in spite of everything we were fond of them. Do we think of them as a futile memory of the life we should have lived rather than that we have actually lived, are we attempting, by our lenience to our clothes to prove ourselves worthy of the splendid costume, the starring role we never had—and which must surely still be waiting for us somewhere? Are we, through our clothes, paying homage to some unknown individual rather than to the person we were born to be, whose place we would usurp, so that we might belatedly be forgiven for our life and for the happiness which, in spite of everything, we feel simply by existing?

Running for the Train

For Bruno Grégoire

IT IS ALWAYS HUMILIATING to run for a train, we are fated to miss it: we will never again take it. When, on the other hand, we do manage to catch it, it is not a simple stroke of luck. With an innocent expression, we step into a compartment and place our suitcases on the luggage rack, attempting to conceal the lingering panic in our breathing from those present; and yet we know that winning the race straight away will bring us greater luck on our journey. Even compared to those worthy souls who took their seats on time.

The Suitcase

When our suitcase leaves us, carried off by a hotel porter, by the conveyor belt at an airport check-in desk, our gaze goes with it as though it carried with it some part of us. When, later, it comes towards us, out of the depths of a left-luggage office or in the arrivals hall of some other airport, we recognise it, greet it straight away though with mixed feelings. Although it seems the same, it is not, the journey it has endured without us is all the more worrying for the fact that it has left it apparently unmarked. But sometimes, later on, spilling our belongings from our suitcase, we find a hairpin we have never seen before; empty, it rings only faintly with the echo of distant laughter. True, it also travels in our stead, serves as an itinerant home, as a black box through which we can journey to otherwise inaccessible places. Alas we cannot guess what hands have rummaged through it, touching—for long minutes perhaps—our comb, our cigar, our pencil with impunity; cannot know what embraces, what assaults by ghastly porters on obscene pencil-thin blondes it has witnessed in the darkness of the baggage hold. In vain do we now observe it from a distance, standing in a deserted doorway in a city we are passing through; once more, we will not come to know our phantom doppelganger to whom we proffer the suitcase like bait, ready this time perhaps to let him have it. It only remains now for us to come back and collect it, reconciled once more to dragging it behind us, to being our own valet.

The Novel

Ceaselessly roving, in the twists and turns, of writing your novel.

Goodbyes

THERE IS A GLORY TO GOODBYES made on a railway platform, but they are best not drawn out. All too quickly they become little more than self-conscious standing around. Whether on the platform or on the train, we freeze into cardboard cut-outs, as do the friends who stand facing us, smiling idiotically for a photograph no one ever takes. In fact, we are no longer really with our friends, any more than they are with us; they will come back only with the secret scrap of paper resting on the railway tracks after they have gone, only when we begin to affectionately bitch about them as we leave the station. For their part, they will be borne away only by chance silhouettes espied standing guard over a bridge behind the station. The inchoate wave or the short nervous laugh with which one of us accompanies his untimely leave-taking from this place of safety sometimes, at a stroke, manages to pierce far into the future and there, in advance, causes our meeting to come into bud in a new chapter of the novel which moves forward relentlessly.

The Firework and the Lightning Flash

We ran to the bend in the road to see the cyclists, but through the trees we saw no more than a brief flash of multicoloured jerseys and glittering spokes. It is the same with fireworks; having rushed to the brow of a hill, to the top of the stairs, we glimpse only a handful of sparks above the rooftops; only as we were coming around a high bend on the ring-road did the firework appear before us in all its glory. That rare and little known lightning in the form of a sphere is a blazing bowling ball stubbornly scouring the distant darkness of the backrooms of the world. Even those seekers whose home it enters through the office window usually turn belatedly to look, as it disappears again, into the outside world, into the night.

The Green and the Blue

For Standa

GREEN AND BLUE SEEM INCOMPATIBLE, as the Czech saying goes, green with blue is good for fools. The real problem, however, is to know how to distinguish between them since at the limits of their range, they have a tendency to merge: grass green shaded with blue, the blue-green of the evening sky, the greeny-blue of the sea. The two colours eyeing one another jealously, keeping a close watch on each other, insisting on their disparity. Blue endlessly proliferates, every painter has a blue particular to him, as though each individual act of seeing is matched by a different tone. Green, on the other hand, keeps itself to itself, to a few elemental shades: bottle-green, the baize green of a billiard table, the green of old bonnets and of greenhouses, the moss green of wallpaper in bars. And yet deep within green gleams a secret snare, a will-o'-the-wisp, a primordial fluorescence, the emerald of a poison ring. Green is the very colour of mystery, its poetic symbol while in blue, from the indigo of night to the azure of morning, there is only a fleeting suggestion of mystery, nothing more than a metaphysical symbol. Where green encourages us to trust, to sink into it as into a swamp, blue demands that we set off to meet it.

The Week

From earliest childhood, the days of the week can be distinguished each by a different destination and colour, though set against the same flaking greyness of the week. Whether washed by the rain or lit by the sun, the colours of the days remain the same, Monday's sand, Tuesday's crushed brick-red, Wednesday's pale gravel-grey are merely more brilliant or more drab; nor do they change much with the passing hours, the shade of early morning, the brightness of afternoon. The days, however, secretly swap places and roles until suddenly we discover that they have perfidiously been replaced by one another. Sunday, white but desolate is nothing but a flawed Saturday, Wednesday despite its paler shade of grey is a Saturday appearing unexpectedly in mid-week; the real Sunday only reveals itself on Monday evening, when restaurants and cinemas remain silent but the eyes of their customers begin to shine once more in the darkness. The rank of the day of silence, which long ago seemed to fall to Wednesday (or, when mingled with a soft drizzle, to Thursday) now definitively falls to Tuesday, nestling quietly beneath the shoulder of the week.

Sunday

1

FROM EARLIEST CHILDHOOD, we found Sunday awkward, gaping before us like an emptiness in the week, like a brusque silence in the human murmurings of the world, that we do not quite know how to fill. The moment we sit down to eat, in spite of a slight stiffness, is still solemn with the anticipation into which we are plunged by the tantalising aromas wafting from the kitchen. We enjoy the meal, the general relaxation it brings; but coffee when it arrives is merely a vain attempt to postpone the inevitable, for hardly have we taken a first sip when we are forced to ask ourselves the crucial question: what do we do now? The party atmosphere fades, disperses in the silence of the sitting room to which we now retire, attempting as best we can to make it feel lived in, in the company of our prim and proper guests—unless, led into some over-polished living room, it is we who, in turn, become stiff and starched. And things are little better when we go out, when we hobble half-heartedly along the deserted streets, past shop windows, their shutters closed, or elbow our way through the crowd at the ticket desk of some museum; everywhere we go, we shiver against the cold, the emptiness of Sunday sets us apart from those with whom we came out just as surely as it does from the strangers who crowd about us. The best way to protect yourself from this emptiness is to withdraw to the kitchen as soon as lunch is finished, and set about doing the dishes, slowly rinse them of the leftovers of the feast, adding to the chink of tableware a few trifling remarks of no great seriousness. As we restrict ourselves to patiently clearing up, the gentle whisper of scenery being shifted pacifies us, the monotony of the task soaking up the thrill of the party and dousing our fears with the imminent bustle of Monday.

We only perhaps truly enjoy Sunday in late morning, when, as we wait for lunch, we make a few phone calls to friends and acquaintances. Through the open window the sputter of breaded escalopes being grilled reaches us, children's cries and the mollifying calls of their parents, for now, the day is simply weighing up its chances, lazily stretching in the pleasantly balmy air. Our friends, for their part, are rested and relaxed, conversing with us at length, attentive and yet casual, asking our advice about possible outings, meetings, lectures, while behind their backs mothers and wives are setting the table. We simply exist, united and yet each man for himself, but this is enough to make us happy; together, we all go on living—almost all of us—together, we still make up the world.

2

The terror which immobile Sunday filled us with as children was also a truth which one day we would have to make our own. The white cage of Sunday, so enticing after the auspicious grey of Saturday, opened inwards as far as the eye could see, like the wasteland which was our childhood and the cold war which was life itself, the seeming emptiness of high days and holy days was simply a precursor of the emptiness that awaited us in the outside world, teaching us how to face it. In vain did we retreat to our childhood dens, coaxing our cousins into playing hide-and-seek; what was important was there before our eyes, in the icy brilliance of the day, between the hats and the stuffy figures of the grown-ups in their Sunday best.

It is something we would truly accept when far from everyone we know, in a foreign city where it might help us settle in. There is nowhere left to run, we are irrevocably *here*. We need only turn away from an empty page and glance towards the deserted boulevards, taking in a vista which stretches away to some distant sea, to inhabit this Sunday setting; similarly, merely thinking of loners in their distant attic rooms peoples the room in which we find ourselves, together with the solos that long-dead jazzmen address to us from a record. We even travel the world more widely without ever leaving home; a simple Sunday walk beyond the ring-road, wandering between the stalls of a flea market, allows us to arrive back in these streets as though returning from some distant city.

Spain and Italy

TIME WAS YOU BAULKED AT ITALY'S CHARMS; Spain alone, arid and austere, seemed to you to be the true South, worthy of your need to sense the mystery of the world. Nothing seemed mysterious but for the crackle of unfamiliar flashes in the darkness of heavily-guarded warehouses, the bulls' panicked breathing behind the boards of their pens, the bleeding viscous casks half-glimpsed in seedy *fondas* with beaten earth floors. Only little by little did the mulishly tenacious *fondas* and cellars withdraw to the margins while the translucency of Italy, of its palazzos and its faded pediments—visible to the whole world—with a barely abstracted brightness, became increasingly compelling—as though the heart of mystery was suddenly coming to the surface here in the clear light of day. Henceforth, you will know that it is not necessary to seek out the dark corner where, with a rush, you feel the knifepoint slide against your skin; to suffer requires little more than a shaft of early spring sunlight cut through with a chill which wraps itself inside the scarf around the neck of elegant young men chatting on the fringes of a *mercato*, whose gesticulating hands, with the speed of experts, carve up the firm young flesh of the light.

The Boat and the Puddle

They rented us a rowboat and, with their help, we step aboard and test it just as the boat in turn tests us; it rolls slightly, pitches underfoot, instinctively we adjust our balance careful not to overdo it so as not to get a soaking at the outset. Meanwhile, we have left terra firma far behind, a pool of water lies in the bottom of the boat. We have not yet sat down and already we have made a journey, perhaps even, in miniature, the entirety of the voyage on which we are embarked.

While bathing in a tranquil lake, we need only swim to the centre to find ourselves surrounded by infinite space. The shore from which we set out is fading into the distance and we cannot yet see the far shore; the silence that enfolds us, barely broken by the drone of an invisible mosquito, stretches endlessly into the cosmos. In the sea, on the other hand, we barely manage to get wet; hardly have we tried to dive in when a treacherous wave looms and the sea pushes us back towards its shore. Its sprawling expanse will never be more to us than a doubtful legend of which we have savoured only a little salty sip.

The lake is wider than the sea as though it alone were the true ocean. We wonder, too, where the depths are: as children, at the swimming pool, we brazenly ventured beyond the shallow end and were disappointed to find that we could still touch the bottom. The only thing which might shed a little light on such things is the story of the captain who, having sailed the seven seas unscathed, died on his way back from a bar—a few feet from his home—face down in a puddle.

The Sea, The Mountain

For Michel Le Guével

EVEN HIGH IN THE MOUNTAINS, something in the landscape suggests the sea; as we look down into the depths of a valley, the shrubs and trees which catch our eye on the slopes, shoring up our gaze, seem like preliminary sketches of the heaving breakers, the salt spray of some distant shore. It is difficult, however, to imagine the sea evoking the mountains (except at the microcosmic level of the waves) since, ever true to itself, it persists in stubbornly ruminating on its own vastness, its essential but insipid enigma. It might be said that it is our taste for metaphor which brings us to the mountains, while we go to the sea to experience life and its mystery in all their literality.

And yet it is true that an expanse of water alone opens out before a house an *other* space, an elsewhere by its very nature different from here and impossible to inhabit unless perhaps by sounding it, an onslaught of thought and vision constantly recommenced from afar; and yet at the same time this elsewhere, whose shore literally grazes the threshold of our home, seems within reach. And so, the more the actual space of our existence shrinks, the more attractive is the presence of a sea, a lake outside our window, offering us both an image of the unknown to which we will one day return, and the murmuring sounds of the Whole, familiar yet impossible to comprehend, which will survive us here.

The Tree, The Path

THERE ARE THREE THINGS we never tire of looking at, things which—like food for the eyes—never cease to soothe us: waves breaking, the flickering of firelight, the leaves of a tree ruffled by the breeze. All three show the world as a constant metamorphosis, and an eternal return, reminding us that we are but a part of its nameless unfurling, and immediately gather us into the warp and weft of it. The tree, moreover, is a singular being, at once the rustling substance of existence and an unknown divinity. Impersonal as well as paternal, it looks at us in each of its leaves without looking at us, and in doing so protects us—heals us. For our part, in return, we examine it within and without, haunt it and inhabit it, both nowhere and everywhere.

The path is content to follow us as we walk; when we cross it, we are merely a glorious movement from one nowhere towards another, the oval of the cycle track unrolled into a straight line. We move from tree to tree like a baton in a relay and between the dead trees that form a guard of honour, the next disaster comes towards us with the murmur of the treetops and just as quickly dies away to become a soothing echo. We can hear all the more clearly the rumbling of the machine that is us, knowing as we have never known that we are here only to make it possible for the world to look upon itself through our eyes.

Seeing

For Tomáš Fragner

LATER, WHEN THE WATERS RECEDED, a friend tells us, the sun began to burn again and I was able to look out on a landscape split in two as in a nightmare: from mid-way up the slope to the summit, lush meadows in flower beneath a luminous sky—and below, nothing but dead, blackened, fetid things, decaying ruins, felled trees. The world as it appears to us every day, but which our friend has suddenly seen.

Boredom

ONLY IN INDOLENCE do we come close to God—and resemble him—assuming the right to waste time which he jealously denies us. Idleness is a luxury, it releases our being in the pure state, suddenly free of the deluge of work, of efforts, of duties to be performed, in the image of the inert substance of which we are wriggling shoots. Idleness, a period spent in and with boredom: the more we languish and stand gaping, the more we plunge into the nature of the thing itself, stirring it within us just as primordial matter did before deciding, in a fit of boredom, to beget us and amuse itself awhile with our comings and goings. We in turn find in boredom something of that first oneness, and tautologically explore it from within, hoping to discover everything and nothing in particular, making out opportunities all around without allowing ourselves to be tempted by any one of them. All you need do is watch Laurel on his own, without Hardy, in the cabin aboard a boat for a moment; first he starts to cry, then he's sporting an idiotic grin; he only has to look at a knot in a plank of wood and immediately he scratches his head utterly baffled. There can be no doubt that at that moment he is so *magisterially* bored, he is godlike.

Clearly, an aptitude for boredom is a skill which must first be acquired, for it is not something bestowed on everyone. The most important thing is to be patient with boredom, to accept it as stroke of luck and not to shirk it, or worse be driven by boredom to doing something else. Do not allow yourself to be bored by it, but embrace it, allow it to unfurl through the honest inner whirling with which it encircles us. Give no thought to digging the allotment or writing a poem, do not struggle needlessly, we should not stint ourselves, on the pretext of being set free, from what little is given us. Simply vary the way in which you swirl the ice-cubes in your glass a little, let your eyes linger for a moment on the title of a book you will not open. It goes without saying that we will be punished for this; any society which ever attained the subtle art of boredom must perforce have perished. Nowadays, even in isolated villages, a poster appears before the holidays in which local entertainers warn: "This summer, you won't manage to be bored." We must once again be subjugated, brought to heel and submit once more to our jealous masters.

Smoking

WHEN THE GUNFIRE HAD CEASED and the two ringleaders found themselves alone in the palace of the conquered Tsars, now suddenly infinitely desolate, even Lenin—a non-smoker—asked Trotsky for a cigarette. It provided him with the only possible prop that made it possible for him to be distracted and yet focused, diverted his attention from his doubts, momentarily set the uncertainty of the moment to one side allowing him, in the midst of the chaos, to revel in being here. While he is smoking, we can feel a certain kinship with Lenin, for he is part of the chain which, running parallel to hostile History, we form with all the unknown smokers to whom we silently offer a light, in a train or at a bus stop at night.

Nor do we fraternise any less with our anonymous partners-in-crime whose glowing cigarettes encircle us, at night, on a public square; what makes our night somehow deeper—and renders our pleasure in tobacco more grave—is the Pall Mall slowly savoured by the parachutist who has landed in virgin forest dangling from a tree. As we stub out our cigarette and leave the square to go inside; the customer, cigarette in hand, standing outside a nearby hotel happily goes on smoking for us and making the world more fit to live in.

The world is sometimes a little overpopulated, the ashtray, in the centre of a rowdy *brasserie*, overflowing and unwilling to accept our butts—driving us out of the place—too little like the great cauldron which once upon a time stood in the middle of the London Stock Exchange waiting for the butts of merchant bankers' cigars. Which made one want to cross the Channel simply to see it; simply to stand before the cauldron and listen as with a mute roar it welcomes this shower of cigar-end shooting stars is enough to make us feel that we have arrived somewhere.

In the primeval world, from what we have glimpsed, there reigned the half-light of a human aquarium; some strolled idly through it, a white thermometer in their mouths, others held forth, brandishing a pipe, still others draped themselves in cigar smoke and loftily dwelt in offices, in chambers and consulting rooms as in shrines to their own divinity. People were particularly diligent at smoking in movies, black and white films being a vast smoking room into which each character brings to his portrayal his own brand of cigarettes, his personal manner of smoking; everyone is deep in thought, sucking on a cigarette, pacing the room, puffing out clouds of smoke and gesticulating, stabbing out a half-smoked cigarette and immediately lighting another as if to prove to us that the world is a place of hustle and bustle in which at every moment, something of great importance is happening. Even on the silver screen it sometimes happened that a man would hit another man, sending his cigarette flying, or corner the man such that, his hand trembling uncontrollably, he drops the cigarette himself. The rift widened during the war, in the dim light of the camps, where some could come by tobacco only by humiliating scrabbling around, while others wore cigarettes on their lips like an arrogant emblem of their power.

The country in which we grow up resembles an immense prison; those who linger, smoking, on the edge of the desert cling to their cigarette as to a buoy and already they have learnt to palm it in front of the screws; it is true that it matters to them all the more. The worst, Ossip remarked in neighbouring Russia, were those who, during routine searches persuaded us to give up tobacco, offering us sweets instead. Some, unfortunately, will surrender of their own free will; it takes only the hint of a promotion to feel compromised both by the cigarette and by the decision to enjoy it. Among those who fail to withstand the ordeal are a good number who gallantly contribute to filling the communal ashtray in a *brasserie*; as soon as they step outside the bar, however, they weaken, beating themselves up about every drag. It is only a matter of time before they agree not to leave their own home and smoke on their doorstep, pilloried before all the world—duly labelled with a badge on the lapel of their dismal jacket. The ashtray in the London Stock Exchange, too, will one day disappear and the proverbial London pea-souper will vanish shortly afterwards. Has the good Lord, himself an inveterate smoker,[12] finally forsaken us?

Thankfully, we still have each other; you smoke one cigarette after another, growing old, honestly suffering the torments of the world and of yourself—and I stand beside you, against the screws and label-wearers, against the good Lord. I espouse your cause and help you to live in the twilight world so assiduously that sometimes, before I have finished a cigar, I have an overwhelming urge to light another.

The Last Drop

From every apparently empty wine bottle, it is possible to wring no fewer than thirty-two drops, according to experts; one need only take the time. It is true—they add—that between the penultimate and the last drop, it is sometimes necessary to wait for six hours; almost enough time for an entire possible life to leach away somewhere. Now, as we finish our drinks, you and I, as we hold the neck of the bottle over the glass listening intently, a little further on we are loving for the last time; but before setting down the bottle, empty now, our lives our boundless and our love infinite.

Vin de Nuit / Night Wine[13]

For Ivan Schneedorfer

WINE, BY ITS VERY NATURE, is not truly a metaphysical drink since it is not transparent. Whereas a drink of water or a glass of spirits immediately get straight to the point, runs through us, their liquid tracer reminding our body of its existence, wine insists, clings to the palate and demands that we tarry over this charming anecdote, its savour. It is altogether too seductive, its fragrant mantle clothes the tongue—and the world—to such an extent that it consumes us, causing us to forget our nakedness as strangers faced with the nakedness of things.

There is, however, one exception: the everyday wine—the Bergerac or the Minervois from the local cellar—which we drink late into the night, making conversation sitting in silence listening to records, all the better to become one with the night. An unassuming social tipple chosen less for its brilliance than for its steadfastness—and sometimes its tenacity—it is a wine which seldom flaunts itself; though it may bring overtones of oxidised metal to the surface, as though to reassure us of its presence, it also blends into the nameless mass, the cool of the surrounding darkness: reveals itself beneath its red flame to be of solid black. One might say it gathers the night into its depths, though, little by little, those depths are eclipsed by simple blackness, shot through here and there by shadowy trains and lustrous dogs.

Fire

WHEN A FIRE BURNS IN THE NIGHT, we have to go, you say—and once again you are right. Fire is a signal which demands a response, a signal by which we should allow ourselves to be guided; it tells us that something is happening in the world and insists that we go and see for ourselves, even if we should find only a lone, silent security guard. We seek out fire like a secret burning of existence, we want to touch it, to see whether the ashes of the charred fields, the burnt-out brickyards we pass on our walks still hide some smouldering ember. Already, we have spotted the flames and quicken our pace, perhaps we will even get to see our own house burn; no, we cannot possibly miss that, everyone is rushing towards the fire, everyone will be there, even children and firemen. No doubt we shall find there many unfamiliar co-conspirators, we need only turn around and study the faces lit by the fire at our back.

Couples

For Nicole Espagnol and Alain Joubert

WE OBSERVE OTHER COUPLES out of the corner of our eye, surprised by their myriad combinations: a radiant effervescent girl with a dreary technocrat, a simpleton with the face of an angel and a woman as ugly as sin, a visionary dwarf and a stupid lion-tamer. It is all very well to say that with the technocrat, the girl need no longer want for anything, that she is all the more radiant for his dreary companionship, or that the ugly woman is a blessing to the simpleton; their being together still unsettles us like the disappointing end to a movie. On the other hand, what people call 'beautiful' couples seem to us to be too showy, as though they were constantly performing, as though they existed only on stage. Others seem to have been brought together by a mutual shade of grey and their willingness to wear it in the rain. Otherwise, we might think that they are always vaguely wondering why they are still together, that they go into their relationships armed with a knife, sharing both their cloak and the regret that the only thing they love in one another is an imperfect world. Whereas the beautiful couple have a photographer with them even in bed, so that with a flash he can immortalise their lovemaking; our two partners rest in silence in the half-light, through the window one sees a crow approaching, the other the water rising. In the middle of the bed, only their hands touch, making love in their stead.

Sometimes, after lovemaking, they turn away from each other, she constantly haunted by the vision of another life, he now suddenly alone again. While she allows herself to be caught up in a first dream, his gaze alights on the breeze rustling the leaves of the trees outside, fleetingly relieving the world of its gravity.

The Crowd

THE CROWD OF VISITORS and inhabitants in a city is not simply an anonymous mass, but an inexhaustible wardrobe of other lives, other potential partners each of whom, from a safe distance, we consider and try on. In this manner during one journey on the metro, we may mentally live out a whole series of embraces, marriages and divorces. Surging out of the depths of the crowd the world presents us with new heroes and their stories to slip into its travelling show—well-worn star turns featuring us and our friends—the unfamiliar tales of a larger-than-life fat man, a smoker with a nervous tic, a crazy singer. Swept up in a crowd, dutifully inching forwards, we can feel the pulse of a foreign city until an untied shoelace forces us to step to the edge of the pavement where we find only drunks and street-hawkers, our secret co-conspirators, standing about in the doorways. As we lean down to tie our shoelace, lifting our foot onto a step or the sill of a shop window, we feel a relief to find ourselves in solidarity only with the stone—still radiant with heat—beneath the sole of our shoe. Shortly afterwards, sadly, we will die in any case unnoticed among the marching imbeciles, and amid the cries with which they seek to deafen themselves.

The Secret Network

For Christian Doumet

As we take our seat at a café table where we have a rendezvous, the waiter comes over and discreetly informs us that there is a telephone call for us: the caller asks us to wait, he is running a little late. Although our meeting is entirely innocuous, the message and the secrecy with which it is imparted gives us the sudden impression of being connected to a secret network in the sprawling city—one otherwise impossible to access—some clandestine order. An impression so exhilarating, we think, that it suddenly explains the behaviour of other people in other cafés who have received phone calls. Do they not also struggle to hide their excitement rather than foolishly draw attention to themselves? One thing is certain: as they get up from their table, all eyes are on them, watching as they cross the café to the telephone; for us, the outsiders, they belong to some secret urban network, and at that moment we might envy them, not simply their imaginary importance, but the fact that for an instant they are strangers to themselves.

The Countryside

For Pavel Kolmačka

IN MANY PEOPLE, the countryside inspires only fear, even those who go there for a short break immediately leave for fear, they say, of being bored. But is that the real reason? Is the risk of boredom what distinguishes the country from the city, the quiet breathing of its trees from the bewitching glimmers of city neon? After all, even they gracefully glimmer through the leaves of the dark treetops; the silence that engulfs us in the midst of a crowd weighs on us more heavily than the silence of the deep forest. Therefore the real reason the countryside inspires fear is because here we cannot hide in the face of a truth which the neon of the city, like a protective shield, protects us from but which in the countryside is displayed in all its nakedness. No, it is not that there is something missing here, it is worse—here we are confronted by what truly exists, the wind and the blind grass, suffocating, teeming with strange noises and chirruping, a stifling heat and a cold that cuts to the bone, the stone walls saturated with rain, the solitude of bodies, the passing of time and beneath it, the unfathomable silence.

Scaring Each Other

TOGETHER, WE WILL SLIP INTO THE ATTIC SPACE, at night, behind the sloping roof, we are going to scare each other. You'll go for me with daddy, I'll parry the blow with mummy, we'll whisper until we're out of breath, our soft murmurs slipping right through the thicket; we will touch a frog and show each other a pale moon, we will shudder at the sight of a shadow near the tree and a bright sheet of paper, blank and deathly pale. We will run away, we will hide from ghosts and grown-ups, laughing at their catcalls, at their distant salvoes, at the creaking of a rusty pump. We will set out animals on the lawn as guards and look out for each other; I'll pop up in front and play the Alpine huntsman, you'll scream in fright, I'll be happy. You'll hitch up your shirt and smile at me in the half-light, you'll take my hand and hold it before my eyes, I'll tumble down in terror, into the depths of the hideaway.

Naked

Naked; you were naked, it was drawing near as when a classmate, his mouth split by a huge smile, runs through the streets shouting that we're going to see you stark naked. The first post-war train pulled noisily into the station, the whimpering of the wounded and the laughter of the strapping stretcher-bearers, it whips up dust and a scrap of newspaper, then suddenly everything is plunged into silence, the scrap of newspaper falls back onto the platform, we wait in vain for what comes next while naked and terrified, crouched somewhere behind a low wall, you hide from witnesses and from yourself.

When do women truly undress? Perhaps you were naked when you found yourself alone in the gentle rumbling, unfamiliar with your secret strength, huddled in a corner or sitting on a toilet bowl where you could be exposed only by an aerial attack bringing the walls of the building tumbling down—like the guy in the old joke, chain in hand, astonished to find that he has brought the house crashing around him simply by flushing the toilet. But nothing of the sort happened, for years, all of you simply washed and pampered yourselves in secret, in the bathroom, as though seeking to cleanse yourselves of yourselves. The cool fresh treasure of perfumes, curves and tufts, of the cleft which later you eventually offered up for our exploration, hid you like some dazzling but deceptive finery.

Time, happily, did not stand still, even now it continues to pass, from the horizon comes the rumble of an approaching storm, little by little by dint of caresses you emerge, your thighs give off a scent of ozone and flare with the glow of phosphorous, suddenly beneath your skirt you are wet in mid-afternoon, in advance as though undressed; caught in the act in the midst of trying on a pillbox hat, in the midst of a race played out along the clattering awnings of the shops, between a disastrous outing and a successful trip, in the course of ever more desolate nocturnal embraces, undressed a little more by each salvo on the outskirts of the city, by each ache in your hips and each bombed out tower on the horizon, you are always within reach, always there, almost naked.

TRANSLATOR'S NOTES

1 John Cornelius 'Johnny' Hodges (25 July 1907–11 May 1970) an American alto saxophonist and lead player of Duke Ellington's saxophone section.
2 Possibly a reference to '*L'Étrangère*', a poem by Andonie Georges *(Les yeux tombeaux sans fond de ton brillant regard)*.
3 In English in the text.
4 Buster Keaton in *The High Sign* (1921).
5 Impossible to translate: while this translates *à moitié chien ... à moitié loup*, it cannot translate the fact that *entre chien et loup* means twilight.
6 Roy Owen Haynes, an American jazz drummer.
7 *Charlot* in the French. Král is referring to the film *A Night Out* (1915).
8 In *Shoulder Arms* (1918) Charlie goes into his dugout, now flooded, and lies down in his waterlogged bunk plumping up his sodden pillow. The only light is from a candle floating on a piece of wood and Charlie pushes it along to singe his comrade's foot, which is hanging over the bunk. Using a gramophone horn as a snorkel Charlie goes to sleep under water.
9 This doesn't work in English—in French *déçu* is almost homonymous with *dessous*.
10 Král is clearly referring to *Vánoí Rybí Polévka*, Czech Christmas Fish Soup, traditionally served in homes at six pm on Christmas day.
11 The references are probably to jazzmen Keith Jarrett (pianist), and Stewart Slam (bassist).
12 Possibly a reference to Serge Gainsbourg's song '*Dieu, fumeur de Havanes*'.
13 *Vin de nuit* is a technical term referring to a rosé wine macerated for only one night, long enough to pick up the colour and tannins from the grape skins.

The author would like to thank Michel Le Guével for his thoughtful attention with which he read the manuscript of this book, and for his invaluable advice.

The translator would like to express his thanks to Hervé Ferrage and Sophie Cauchy of the Ambassade de France à Londres for their support, and to Guy Walter, Cédric Duroux, Adélaïde Fabre, Isabelle Vio and Emmanuelle Bellissard for all their kindness during his brief but memorable residency at the Villa Gillet in Lyon while translating Notions de base.